MIRACLES ARE NORMAL

69 Stories Of Divine Interventions And Magical Manifestations

SOUL PURPOSE
PUBLISHING

Other Multi-Author Books By Soul Purpose Publishing

My Mess Is My Message

Success With Source

My Mess Is My Message II

I'm So Glad You Left Me

Divine Rebirth

CONTENTS

My Miracle Children

Dina Marais

I have experienced many miracles in my life and many I am sure I don't even remember. My birth was a miracle because I died and was brought back to life. I was clearly meant to be here!

Each of my children had an accident that could have cost them their lives. These miracles showed not only that they were meant to be here too, but that they came away unscathed.

It was a Friday afternoon. My husband, Johan, had returned from work and we were getting ready to visit friends. We were chatting away in our bedroom while he was getting dressed. Suddenly, my husband said, "Where's Nadia?" She wasn't around us. I called her name, thinking she must be somewhere close. No answer.

The most dreadful fear filled my whole body. I ran down the passage and screamed her name. Then I heard soft splashing. She was in the pool, lying on her back - only her little face was visible. Her lips were blue. I screamed for my husband. I yanked her out and he grabbed her. We frantically called the doctor. Fortunately, he was still in the consulting rooms.

Nadia was just over a year old and had managed to open the gate that led to the pool. We thought it was secure. My husband said that the moments it took to run down the passage to the pool were the worst, not knowing what he was going to find.

When we arrived at the doctor's rooms, my parents-in-law were waiting for us. They lived just down the road. The receptionist was an old friend and had called them. Nadia was fine. No water had entered her lungs. But my husband was prescribed some tranquilizers. He was in a terrible state. The possibility of losing her was too much. After that, he became paranoid for a while, calling me ten times a day to check where Nadia was. Needless to say, we installed a net to cover the pool.

About 7 years later, we made some renovations to our home. We converted an open space between the main house and the cottage where my parents-in-law stayed, into a covered parking space. Part of this project was a new 10-foot iron gate. When the gate was delivered that week, it took ten burly men to offload it from the truck and place it on its track. We were waiting for the gate motor to be installed. In the meantime, the building contractor put a pile of rubble at the end of the gate to stop it from running off its track.

This particular Friday, my husband and I were enjoying a drink to ease into the weekend when we heard our daughter, Nadia, yelling, "Morne is under the gate!" We ran outside to find our son lying on the ground with this huge gate on top of his 5-year-old body. Foam was coming out of his mouth...eyes rolling in his head...I thought he was going to die any second. My husband and father-in-law picked up that gate and put it back on its track in one single movement! We rushed Morne to the hospital and even though they don't do emergencies, they helped him. He had cuts on his head that had to be stitched. He was sent for a brain scan and X-rays. Nothing was broken. He was fine within a few days.

It turned out that the building contractors removed the rubble, not realizing it was stopping the gate; Morne wanted to visit his grandparents, and he wanted to ring the bell. To do that, he had to go out of the big gate. He easily moved the gate which, when it went off its track, fell over.

A few years later, while visiting my mother-in-law in the cottage next door, the next incident occurred that involved Chris. He was about 2 years old at the time. Lettie, my mother-in-law, decided to make coffee for us. While she was pouring the coffee, Chris was standing between her and the counter. He also wanted something to drink and he was impatient like most 2-year-olds. She told him to wait a moment; she just wanted to make the coffee. He wanted her to pick him up, so he was not standing still; he was pushing against her. He turned around to face the counter and that movement caused her arm to catch the mug of hot, black coffee, which fell and poured out onto Chris.

Oh, the agony! The screams! We immediately pulled off his T-shirt and the skin on his little arm came off with it. We rushed to the doctor. With Morne's gate accident, the hospital asked us to go the doctor first and have the doctor warn the hospital. But the doctor was busy with a consultation and she didn't think to check what the problem was. We waited for an excruciating 20 minutes that felt like an eternity.

At the hospital, they treated Chris and dressed the wound. We were instructed to come back the next day. This happened 2 days before we were to leave for our summer holiday.

The following day, when we returned to the hospital, we encountered a miracle. The nurse was an expert in burn wounds, having worked in the burn unit at the Red Cross Hospital. She was very upset about the incorrect way the burn wound was dressed with all that gauze pressing into the flesh. It took her 30 minutes to carefully and gently remove the bandages and apply the proper ointment and fresh dressings.

We went back again the next day and she gave me what I needed to dress the wound myself. Within 5 days Chris's skin was completely healed. He had to wear a hat and long-sleeved T-shirts for 6 months so that his skin was not exposed to the sun. Most of the coffee had fallen on his neck between his head and his shoulder.

And thank his Angels, he had turned his face to the side the moment before the coffee spilled.

These miracles make me think of a passage in the Bible that says, "Not a hair will fall from your head if it is not the will of God." Today all three of my children are amazing human beings and I am honoured for the miracle of being their mother and witnessing their miracles. I know my late husband is watching over us.

Dina Marais - Author, Publisher, Prosperity Alignment Coach
https://www.dinamarais.com
https://www.facebook.com/dinamarais1/

Surrendering To The Miracle Within

Angelique Barlow-Kearsley

If you had told me years ago that miracles would become a way of life for me, I would have laughed, or perhaps even cried at the impossibility of it.

As you see, much of my life has been lived in survival. I grew up in an environment that carried deep trauma—pain, abuse, submission, abandonment and the kind of silence that makes a child feel invisible.

For years, I walked through life dissociated, carrying layers of conditioning that told me I wasn't enough. My nervous system was always braced for impact, and I learned to live small, unseen, and unheard.

And yet, beneath all that pain, there was always a whisper. A quiet knowing that everything is 'going to be ok'. That, there had to be more life. It wasn't meant to be endured, but to be LIVED! That whisper was my Soul, calling me home. I didn't know it at the time, but that was the beginning of my miracle journey.

The first true miracle in my life wasn't something tangible—it was the slow, sacred remembrance of who I really AM. It was the moment I began saying yes to healing, to peeling back the layers of pain, and to reclaim my voice, my worth, and my connection to the Divine.

It was the realization that I wasn't broken, and that I didn't need to earn love. I WAS LOVE! I was already whole. And through this remembering, my Soul was the most profound miracle of all. It opened the doorway to every other miracle that followed.

One of those miracles came in a form I could never have orchestrated on my own. For 2 years, I held a vision in my heart of living on land. I dreamed of wide-open skies, walking barefoot beneath the majestic oak trees and raising my family in a space where we could breathe deeply and root ourselves in nature. I longed for a sanctuary—a place that wasn't just a house, but a home for my Soul.

I leaned into what I had learned from my healing: to trust the unseen, to surrender control, and to believe that if God placed a desire in my heart, there must be a way.

2 years later, 10 acres of land that matched my dream perfectly appeared! Though it required closing within 30 days. Everything about it said "impossible." But instead of collapsing into fear, I chose to trust. I chose to remember that miracles don't follow logic, they follow alignment. I held the vision, prayed over it, and opened myself to divine orchestration.

And then, as only miracles can do, the pieces began to fall into place. Doors opened where there had been none. Resources appeared, paperwork was approved, and within 30 days, we were handed the keys! Our home on 10 acres was delivered in divine timing!

I can still feel the awe of that moment. Walking the land for the first time as its steward, the wind blowing on my face. I fell to the ground and wept! It wasn't just about the house. It was a living reminder that when we align with our soul and surrender fully, miracles meet us in the most extraordinary ways!

What I have learned through both of these stories—the 'Inner Miracle' of Healing and the 'Outer Miracle' of Manifesting our land—is that they are inseparable. The 'Outer Miracle' would never have come if I hadn't first allowed the 'Inner Miracle' to unfold. I had to believe I was worthy of love, peace, and abundance. I had to trust that the same God who was guiding me home to my soul, could also guide me home to the land I longed for.

Miracles are not random, nor are they reserved for a chosen few. They are the natural expression of a life lived in trust, alignment, and surrender. They are the language of the Soul, reminding us that we are not separate from God, but deeply woven into the fabric of Love itself.

As I look back now, I see that miracles are not extraordinary events at all—they are what happens when we remember our true nature. When we soften the grip of fear, when we dare to dream, when we lean into love instead of lack, the miraculous becomes normal.

And that is my deepest prayer for any soul reading these words. To know that your life, too, is a field of miracles waiting to bloom. To trust that even in the darkest moments, something beautiful is being born. To believe that the desires in your heart are not foolish—they are the voice of your soul, guiding you home.

Because miracles are not something that happens to us. They are something that awakens within us. And when they do, your life will never be the same.

Angelique Barlow-Kearsley - Intuitive Guide and Soul Energy Initiator

https://www.instagram.com/abundantmoon111

https://www.facebook.com/abundantmoon111

Let's Go Home

Ann Jonas

This story exists because I chose to trust in Me and in God...

It was the path that was meant to be taken. My daughter and I were living in California where we were both born and raised. We needed to leave our home state due to our lifestyle not being aligned with the state's guidelines/beliefs. Her medical exemption would not work once it was time for her to start 7th grade. I had already witnessed many families leaving the state for similar reasons, aka medical freedom.

I made a friend when I was pregnant, and we gave birth to our kids one day apart. We raised them with similar views on health and wellness, parenting style and spiritual beliefs. We ran into each other one day, essentially at the end of the Covid pandemic era. She told me about their family's upcoming move to Idaho. She had done the research, looked at every state in the Nation to decide where her family should be, to have the lifestyle that aligns with their personal beliefs.

Trusting the path in front of me, we had a year to go and my plan was that I would put my house on the market, sell it, qualify for a mortgage, find a house in Idaho and move in July so that my daughter would have the summer to get acclimated in her new home.

The first step was to take a trip to Idaho and check out the town that our friend had chosen. That October my daughter and I took a road trip to see our new home state and where our friend had moved to. We loved it and we were ready to put our move out of state into planning. I met my realtor; she set me up on the MLS and that was that. The plan was in motion. Over the next few months, I enjoyed seeing the properties that were available in our chosen town and getting a lay of the land.

When I told people of my plan, I loved hearing how many people thought that I was crazy and stupid, that I knew nothing about real estate, managing money, or navigating time. They all said, "Good luck with that."

As the new year dawned, it was time to plant the seed for the sale of my house, starting with the realtor. As a networker by design, I love connecting with people and I had two women in my heart that I energetically felt matched with so I envisioned that I would work with one of them. It was March and one of them sent me a FB message, randomly, asking for a coffee date. I knew this was a Divine alignment and by the end of our coffee, she was my realtor.

We had been living in our house for nine years; it was full of stuff, much of it was not anything that I actually used or needed. We had quite a task ahead of us. It was going to be a miracle to get that house ready for Market.

One night in mid-April, I got a "Divine assignment" that I was to book my plane ticket to Idaho for the next month. I was given specific dates. I listened and my trip to find a house was on the calendar for mid-May.

By May 1st the house was on the market. We had decided on one week of showings and we would get our buyer. On May 9th, I received an offer. It was 25k over asking, 10-day close, no contingences and all-cash. I called my Idaho realtor, and we jumped up and down together. That offer would give me the opportunity to get pre-approved for a mortgage. We would be good to go if there was something to buy when I flew up the following week.

It turned out there were 3 houses in my price range to look at. I landed, got my car and we met at the first house...too small. Off to the next house...too big. Yep, the 3rd house was perfect. That night we were in contract!

As miracles are normal...the inspector that my realtor preferred, happened to have a cancellation and was available the next day.

That house closed on June 14th. I went to sign the papers, staying in my new home on a borrowed air mattress. Six weeks from my house going on the market I took ownership of another home, in another state.

I was 54, our house address was '2016', we had lived there for 9 years. '9' being a number of completions, it was all aligned. That was the last place I would live in California, and we drove away on July 7th, 2023, the 7/7/7 portal.

Trust and synchronicity are the recipe for recognizing that Miracles are Normal.

Ann Jonas aka The Love Messenger – Intuitive Channel and Transformational Guide
https://www.thelotuspath.love
https://linktr.ee/misslotus

Finding Me

Anne Bennet

I was always that girl who never quite fit in anywhere. I was never part of the cool group, and I spent most of my life wanting to be seen. I struggled deeply with my body image resulting in my being bullied throughout most of my school years. It became so overwhelming that I eventually quit school in Grade 12.

For years after that, I worked in a laundromat and a convenience store. I knew I wanted more —more stability, more purpose, and proof to myself that I was somebody. So, I made the decision to go back to school. In my early twenties, I became a Continuing Care Assistant, while working in long-term care.

At that time, I had two children however I was in a mentally and emotionally abusive relationship. When my youngest was just two months old, I left that relationship and I started my life over as a single mother, still working in long-term care and relying on my parents for help with childcare. My family became my greatest support during that time.

Two years later, I met my husband. After only six months, I moved myself and my boys half an hour away from my parents to a small rural village in Musquodoboit Harbour. We blended our families — my two boys and his two girls, who were ten years older than my children. I was incredibly grateful. His parents became

"Nanny and Grampy" from day one, and his sister became "Aunty." I finally felt like I had found another home.

After fifteen years in long-term care, I was able to return to school once again. I graduated with honors in my adult learning diploma and then went on to nursing school. By then my boys were ten and twelve. I worked as an LPN for another ten years, all while navigating profound loss.

In 2015, my mom passed away. It was devastating. My grief eventually pulled me into a deep depression, but I kept going. Two years later, my mother-in-law passed away—another enormous loss for our family. By then, I knew I needed help as I was in a very dark place.

That is when I met an Indigenous clinical social worker who changed my life. She taught me about healing, smudging, patience, self-love and how to express myself. Most importantly, she introduced me to meditation. Through meditation, I discovered that I was connected to Spirit. I had always known I was connected to something more...I just didn't know what that "more" was.

My life started to change. I was connecting to Spirit so often but not realizing it. And then I met Psychic medium Shawn Leonard. He was incredibly accurate - beyond anything I expected. That day, I said out loud that I wanted to do what he did; I wanted to bring to people the peace he had brought to me. Within a week, I heard about a course he offered called Spirit Talker Tribe. I joined without hesitation, without even knowing where the money would come from. I just knew it was meant for me.

Through Shawn's teachings I found myself and finally, my life's purpose! I had found my place; a place where I belonged with no judgment and no bullying. The Spirit family I chose!

One Saturday evening as I was headed to bed, I had a chat with Spirit. If I was meant to be a Spirit Talker, I needed my own space. I needed to be able to stop worrying about where money was coming from. The next morning, I was playing an online game and I won $12, 792.00. They had heard me! This was enough to build my space! I was beyond grateful.

I always trusted that Spirit would give me what I needed. My trust in the spirit world has grown in 8 years. My son was married in August of 2025, and my sister-in-law and I were doing the catering. It was a big expense. 2 days before the wedding, my furnace blew. All I could do was laugh and say, "ok Spirit this isn't funny... now I need the money to pay for a new furnace". Five days later I won 12K on the same game as before. It was enough to pay for a new furnace. I am so beyond grateful.

I now have my own Spirit Shop, The Healing Hut. I work with Spirit through many modalities; Reiki, Human Design, the Akashic records and I host workshops. I get to help people to connect to their loved ones on the other side and I help them through their grief. I can never nurse again but I can still help.

It may have taken me a while, but I have finally found where I fit it and what I am meant to do.

I am a Healer!

Anne Bennet - Psychic Medium

https://www.facebook.com/share/g/1F231kWquj/

My Vipassana Experience

Birgitta Samavarchian

Vipassana is the legacy of Gotama Buddha, who lived 2500 years ago. The word Buddha actually means the enlightened one. Buddha was born to a wealthy family and meditated under a tree in his garden and pondered why it is that people who are rich are just as unhappy as people who are poor. His realization was that it had to do with attachment. Attachment to the things we love, and therefore crave, and attachment to the things we don't like, and therefore develop an aversion to or hate. This creates misery. He had an important realization: Everything in life is temporary. For example, you think you are the same tomorrow as you were today, but meanwhile your body has created a trillion new cells. You cross a river in the morning and at night, and think it is the same river. But a million liters of water have passed, different fish have swum, etc. What Buddha found as a solution to not get into the misery of attachment, was to develop equanimity, a balanced mind.

It turns out that every strong reaction we ever had gets stored in our body. In fact, every trauma, anger, sadness, grief and so on gets manifested in the body as a sensation. And what Buddha realized was that by sitting in silence you can tune into yourself, as opposed to the outside world, and find your own personal truth inside your own body. All these sensations prevent you from happiness, harmony and peace. Layer upon layer they can create both physical as well as emotional pain. But life is to be happy! Suffering is indeed optional.

The Vipassana breathing technique itself is very simple. You sit and breathe in and out through your nose. No counting, no words or mantras. All you focus on is your breath and the triangle under your nose. It is hard to do at first, just like the prolonged sitting in the beginning. You don't only give up your regular life for 10 days, but also your phone, TV, music, books, even paper and pen. You hold noble silence and basically live the life of a nun or monk, surrendering to the process and the rules. You get up at 4 am to meditate and go through meditation throughout the whole day in one-hour increments, broken up by short breaks to stretch your legs and go for a walk. You eat vegetarian food, lovingly prepared by the volunteers, meditate till 9 pm and go to sleep, sometimes emotionally exhausted, at 9:30 pm. Indeed a humbling experience.

Now to my own Vipassana experience: Unexpectedly, the silence was not hard but in fact a relief! There are so many things going on in your head, heart and body, that it would be stressful to try to express what's going on in you. At the beginning my mind was going crazy, it was so busy! Many pictures and unstoppable songs were popping up, but since I was supposed to be in silence, I tried to turn them off. Not a chance, haha! My sense of humor sharpened. In my mind's eye were people I had never seen before, and unknown scenes. It made we wonder if it was from a different timeline, reality or even lifetime. I found it fascinating.

The night of day 3 I heard a rhythmically sounding noise in my ears, and thought, oh, someone must be having a party, with loud music. That's weird, this is such a secluded spot. It must be from a car close by. Then I realized, oh, no, it is my own heartbeat! I called out loud "Hey, slow down, this is too much!" And to my surprise it did! Then all of a sudden, I felt, oh my God, I'm not getting enough air. And then I realized, oh shoot, this is because I told my heart to slow down, and that had an effect on my lungs, too! So I said, come on guys, I still gotta breathe! And it got balanced. This then made me realize that since the body ALWAYS listens, it is SO important to talk to it in an appreciative way and to treat it with love and respect! Also, the body responds when you really tune in! Wow, what a revelation. So I proceeded to talk to all of my organs. This is when I got the intuition that my gallbladder was unhappy with me eating greasy foods! Then I thanked my liver, and announced that I will have warm lemon water every morning, and it started to vibrate happily. I found that so cute and endearing! I fell in love with it right there and then. I had the realization that our bodies incessantly work so hard to renew, repair and to function. It made me see that the core essence in every cell of our bodies is LOVE!! This was very touching to me.

From day 4 on we were instructed to go to the top of our heads and feel the pulsating sensation in what's called the fontanelle in a newborn baby (the upper middle part in your skull that is not completely closed when you are born as a baby). We were then directed to do a body scan with different instructions and techniques every day. The sensation you feel can be like little rivulets or pulsations, or turning energy, or dense sensations. Sometimes it can even feel numb, but if you stay there, you might feel a tiny pulsing underneath that potentially can get stronger. Your task is to just observe, not to go into liking or not liking, just to be the witness and stay with it, with equanimity, a balanced mind. And that is where the magic lies! Because by just being with it, the stuck energy transcends! The sensation dissolves. And you have liberated yourself from the original reaction, the trauma, grief, anger, sadness or whatever else it was. It is a purification of the mind. Personally, I felt my senses getting finer; it gave me laser-sharp focus, a sheer determination and drive I had not known, and a very strong and resonating voice. Giving myself this love and compassion by sitting with the truth in my own body effectively changed my frequency!

One day, I was walking in the mesmerizing enchanted little forest adjacent to the meditation hall, and stood in the sun, and counted up to 12 different areas in my body that either were painful or had discomfort, and felt called to proclaim: Universe, I will stop trying to fight, trying to fix all these things, I surrender them to you. Later that day, in meditation, an energy came over me, that went to all those 12 places, one by one, taking care of, dissolving and healing them! And not only 12, but 15, because I had forgotten a couple! Now this is not the ordinary expectation during Vipassana, but it happened to me several times. I also started to recall how free I felt in my body as a younger person, and this feeling came back and rejuvenated me. At least for a time period, because, *anicca*, everything is temporary! The more you go back into reaction in your everyday life, the more you multiply misery, and might lose what you gained. It is important to continue the daily meditation practice. It is like a sort of maintenance. The practice helps you to retain the happiness, peace and harmony in your body and mind.

One other thing I learned from Vipassana is that when something starts to feel difficult in daily life, it is an opportunity to switch channels. By going into the breath and the sensation, you can override the emotion originating from the mind, and the subconscious conditioned programming of childhood and a lifetime of unconscious reactions. These are based on outdated or false beliefs and stories we have been telling ourselves. I now try to consciously choose between love or fear. Even if I react, it is short-lived. I also attempt to make my decisions from my heart as opposed to my head. I used to be mainly head-centered and a master suppressor of feelings and emotions. This didn't serve me well; I ended up with a 4th-stage cancer diagnosis in 2012. I can now say I am the most authentic and best version of myself. I live the life of my dreams.

Back to my Vipassana retreat: After the 10 days were over, my husband picked me up and told me about the Iran-Israel war that had just broken out, and to my surprise, I didn't react in my usual fashion. Although I felt sorry to hear that people were suffering, it didn't affect me as it would have before going to this retreat. It was like I was tuned into a different wavelength, and didn’t get pulled into the drama. I now know that a vibration of peace, love and compassion does more good than fear, catastrophizing, worrying, hating, wishing bad onto perpetrators, and so on. The latter is actually having the opposite effect. Only 5% of the population can change the vibration of the world for the better. That’s why I try to keep my vibration high at all times. We are presently going through the birthing process for a new earth, a renaissance of sorts, and this will lead to better outcomes for every living being.

My Vipassana experience is just another ordinary miracle. Because miracles are normal.

Birgitta Samavarchian - Certified Life Coach, Healing and Travel Expert
https://www.birgitta-healing.com
https://www.facebook.com/share/1Aqw3VQGZh/

The Universe In A Teacup: Sipping On Small Wonders Of Everyday Life

Birgitta Visser

"Life is a breathtaking miracle and You are a beautiful infinite God Wonder of the I AM in You, as much as the You in the I AM and each other."

The Ascended Master St. Germain

My father always used to say, "You are nature's greatest miracle." He was right. We are. And we will always be the master alchemist of our own lives, weaving the energies as we see fit into existence according to the recipes of the experiences brewed up in our minds.

Instead of being hooked on the worldly acid-tripping-hookah of disinformation that many are so accustomed to, embrace your own 'I AM' Power. We are all diamonds, sparkling with potential, but how can we see the shine if we keep ourselves locked in a drawer?

Even in the darkest of times, when trauma and pain engulfed my soul, I turned to the Universe and my spirit guides for help. As they always say, ask and it is given, just not always in the way you expect. On the first Saturday of 2025, as I walked my farty companion Myra, through the wooded area near my home, I was drawn to look upwards at the still-dark sky. In that moment, a shooting star streaked across the heavens, its luminous trail painting a short, yet unforgettable brushstroke of wonder. Overcome with awe and gratitude, I simply stood there, smiled, and thanked spirit.

Just when we think we've got it all figured out, the Universe throws us a curveball that knocks us right on our arses. But you know what? Sometimes those curveballs are actually miracles in disguise.

Take my experience with my ex for example - and I'm not a fan of labels per se; however, he was what you would call a narcissist who left a trail of destruction in his wake. What can I say? According to my soul contract, he was an agent of chaos, meant to trigger me in so many ways that eventually I would finally see the light of day and heal. Despite having known him for over twenty years, and now not seen him for fifteen, I carry nothing but gratitude that he was a part of my life.

Living with him in my home in the Costa Blanca in Spain for several weeks, turned my tranquil Spanish haven into what felt suspiciously like a direct flight to the lower circles of Dante's inferno. One minute he'd be charming, the next he'd be raging and abusive. He was convinced he had a chip implanted in his head and this belief, coupled with his steroid use and a cocktail of substances, only added to the turmoil. But you know what? He was a magnificent trainwreck and a beautiful reflection. And as painful and traumatic as that experience was, I wouldn't change it for the world. It became a catalyst for my growth, finally shutting the door on the past and releasing the "what-ifs" that had been holding me back.

Healing from that raw, devastating, emotional 'sushi' wasn't exactly a walk in the park with unicorns, but wallowing? Nah, that's just poking the same wound with a stick and expecting it to magically heal. So, I put on my big-girl pants, dragged myself through the darkness and faced those inner demons head-on. Because let's be real, there are no express lanes to healing ourselves, only scenic routes filled with unexpected revelations and the occasional spiritual pothole; and embracing that journey? That is where the true magic lies.

Despite everything that was happening, I never stopped talking to my guides and guardians, including my dad, who had passed away in 1988 from coronary heart disease. No matter how many times I cleansed the toxic vibes from the house I shared with my ex, a lingering residue remained. I remember telling my dad that I wanted to move to Turre, in Almeria, a town set against the backdrop of the Sierra Cabrera Mountains. After a few months, I forgot about my request. Weeks before my lease was up, and after an exhaustive, soul-crushing search for a new place in my current area that felt as wrong as socks with sandals, a completely out-of-the-blue opportunity practically slapped me across the face, with me taking that "cosmic leap of faith." I remember driving into that lush, mountainous embrace with a profound sense of homecoming washing over me—something I rarely experience, as I've moved more times than my age, and I have always been a bit of a nomad. This little voice in my head hinted at me viewing two properties, and sure enough, when I met the Realtor, he said an additional listing had just come onto the market. The first property was a total disaster, with a growing mould garden in the bathroom and a washing machine awkwardly stashed in an overgrown garden. However, when I stepped into the newly built two-bedroom, one-bathroom gem with a skylight, I felt an instant connection. It was like the Universe winked, "see? We told you so!" and I just knew I was on the right path.

Yes, it was a number thirteen house, and before you reach for your lucky rabbit's foot, let's just say my inner numerologist was thrilled. Forget the silly superstition of a skipped thirteenth floor as is often done with buildings and hotels; this was a beacon of creativity and spiritual awakening, not a portal to hell. The detached corner bungalow offered breathtaking views of the mountains, their jagged peaks creating a stunning tableau against the azure, blue sky.

Turre, with its zen atmosphere and unspoiled natural beauty, stood in stark contrast to the tourist-laden streets of Orihuela Costa, where I had spent the past eighteen months. It served its purpose, but it was time to turn the page and embark on a new adventure

In the realm of dreams, my dad popped in with a knowing grin, and I felt a wave of gratitude wash over me. I silently thanked him for leading me to my new home in Turre, fully aware of his guidance and cosmic influence. His eyes twinkled with mischief and love as he returned my smile, a silent acknowledgment of the unbreakable bond we share. Then, out of nowhere, he whipped out a pad and a pen, scribbling away with purpose. I asked him why he was writing when suddenly it hit me: it was my turn to grab my own pad and pen and to dive back into my spiritual journey and channel the wisdom of the Universe once more. I was blown away by the synchronicity of it all. I couldn't help but chuckle at the playful yet profound ways in which our loved ones in spirit communicate with us. Their messages serve as a reminder that the love we share transcends the boundaries of the physical world and that even in the astral planes of our dreams, they are always with us, guiding us and encouraging us to embrace our own divine purpose. How can that not be beautiful?

Two weeks later, after a shit load of organizing, I found myself exactly where I needed to be. We often forget to trust ourselves and the Universe, clinging to control like a toddler with a favorite toy. But when we dare to let go, life flows freely, proving that the Universe has a knack for unfolding in the most miraculous ways.

After a week in my new home, I found myself out walking my dog at the crack of dawn, staring up at a sky sprinkled with stars. Suddenly, a single point of light detached itself from the constellations. It wasn't a star (or Starlink!); it moved with impossible speed and purpose before a second, then a third, winked into existence beside it. They weren't ships of metal, but orbs of soft, pulsating luminescence that moved like a school of fish, darting and weaving in a silent, celestial ballet. One by one, eight of them gathered, their light casting a gentle, ethereal glow. For twenty minutes, I stood transfixed, dog by my side, absorbing the sheer magic of it all.

It reminded me just how vast and mysterious the Universe is. I was in awe and I found myself whispering words of thanks to the Universe, to my spirit guides and to my galactic family for gracing me with their presence and feeling an overwhelming love for the forces that watch over us. I stood as a humble witness to the miracles that dance through our existence, forever changed by the beauty and magnificence of the Universe that embraces us all.

You are truly nature's greatest miracle. You are a cosmic dancer amongst the starlit divine breath of the heavens, having chosen this human experience to shatter your enchanted 'I put a spell on you,' minds, to reawaken the dormant soul and reignite your divine spark, in turn inspiring others to join the transformational dance of life and light up their own brilliance, elevating not only their consciousness, but also that of Mother Earth.

I'm filled with gratitude for the stunning surroundings in which I now find myself. It is a blissful slice of heaven, where I can nurture my soul and deepen my connection to the Universe, all while marvelling at the synchronicities that led me here.

Be grateful for the breath of life and dance with the Universe. Celebrate the journey of your soul and think not so little of yourself, for you are a marvellous, miraculous masterpiece of creation, and a beacon of hope in a world that needs your light.

"You are a delicious burst of dipped in chocolate-covered delight of a light of soul. You are a pistachio in a bowl of nuts, and in a world full of 'pee-nuts', embrace your inner crunchy pistachio, adding sweetened timbres of richness to the collective experience of life.

Never lose sight of the magic you behold within; you are a cosmic traveller housed in a temporary organic earthly suit, gracing the surface of Gaia with your soul presence, learning to dance back to the grid of your whimsical brightness through the created a la carte menu of your experiences."

The Ascended Master St. Germain

Birgitta Visser - Author, Soul Empowerment Coach and Divine Channel

https://www.powersoulhealing.com/

https://www.youtube.com/@powersoulhealing

Wasps Got My Back

Bruce Becker

Prayer is not a one-way street. Prayer is a conversation - if you are open to receive. I often pray while driving and one day as I was telling God how grateful I was for all the blessings in my life, I distinctly heard, 'Gratitude goes both ways.' I had to pull over the car. God, the Almighty, Creator of a Universe vast beyond imagining; God, the Highest Sovereign of all manner of things, spoke to me. There is a saying that I heard from a Muslim friend that goes, "God is closer to you than your jugular vein." God is all around us, in the molecules of the air, the rocks and the trees... and God is listening.

Last summer it became horribly dry in the area where I live. We had no snow the winter before, so there was no snow melt in spring to fuel the plant growth. With weeks of no rain, the scenery began to turn hues of brown. I prayed to God that so long as it did not take needed water from somewhere else, could we please have a gentle soaking of rain for a day or so. I then remembered the scent of electricity in the air from coming rains... I felt the raindrops on my face... the water trickling down my front... I felt the moisture running down between my toes. I was so grateful for it. Please God, let it be so. Amen.

Here in northern Illinois, weather systems usually come out of the west or the southwest, especially in summer. I live in a simple old house, with an old roof, surrounded by half an acre of mature maple trees. The next day, despite weather forecasts predicting clear weather, a freak storm came from the north. The sky turned black that afternoon with intense winds of up to 80 miles per hour, bringing hail and tornadoes in many areas. Branches lurched violently as the air churned through the trees. I parked the car in the garage and settled in for a stormy night. In bed that night, we felt rather than heard a deep thud through the bed as we lay trying to sleep. We woke the next morning, after a noisy night of thunder and wind, to find that a massive branch from the huge maple tree next to the house had broken off in the wind, landing north to south to the side of the house.

If God had answered my prayer for rain and it had approached in a normal pattern, from the west-southwest, that branch, which at its base was wider than I could get my arms around and was about one hundred feet long, would have crushed my house. Because God found the life-giving moisture to the north, the wind broke the branch to fall north to south.

On closer inspection, I noticed a number of smaller branches had fallen on the aging roof. My neighborhood was wrecked with fallen and uprooted trees. News reports came in that a 'bomb cyclone' had hit my area with 100 mph winds exploding in an instant. Anything not secured in the storm was blown around littering people's lawns and gardens. Many streets were closed and traffic lights were not working.

I am too old to be crawling up ladders onto my roof. My guardian angel suggested I call my Homeowners Insurance carrier and ask for an inspection. They sent out a nice man in his late 50's who happily jumped up the ladder with a camera. He said there was damage to some of the roof tiles and that the roof was badly in need of replacement. He didn't need to, but he noted there was a rider on my policy that covered $10,000 in storm damage if the tiles were not manufactured anymore. He suggested I get an estimate, as my roof would not last another storm.

My house is filled with wasps, hornets and spiders of all sorts that live in harmony with me. Milkweed fills my summer backyard, blessing me with ladybugs and

Monarch butterflies. The house may be falling apart but I love it and I started looking for roofing contractors.

The first one was a national brand with a fancy website. They sent out a dark-haired man with white teeth and big muscles in a collared shirt, driving a brand new red truck. We shook hands and he said he would take a look. After a while I went out to find him sitting in the back of his truck nursing his right arm. He had disturbed a wasp while setting up his ladder and it had stung him, so he never did the inspection. But he was more than happy to quote me his exorbitant prices. The wasps were saying, 'not this one.' I phoned a local construction contractor who said he was busy with all the storm damage, but that he would come take a look. I told him my story, that I had $10,000 available to replace the tiles and not much more than that. He responded that he would have to think about it. I gave him the insurance inspector's contact information. He phoned me after about a week, telling me that the baseboards on the roof need replacing, but that he would replace the roof at cost. Not one worker was stung while replacing my roof. God had turned a disaster into an answer to prayer.

Bruce Becker - Prayer Warrior, Storyteller
https://www.facebook.com/groups/899987402858623/about/
https://www.facebook.com/bruce.becker.39006

When The Soul Begins to Remember - A Sacred Witness To The Soul's Journey

Calleen Russell

For many years I sat beside people at the threshold between this life and the next, often in the quiet familiarity of their own homes.

Most people imagine a hospice as a place filled with sadness. And yes, there are tears… goodbyes… There are moments when families struggle to let go of someone they love deeply.

But what I witnessed again and again was something far more sacred. I witnessed the quiet moments when the soul begins to shine through.

Over time I noticed something remarkable. As the body grew weaker and the mind grew quieter, many people began to see or sense things that others in the room could not.

Sometimes a patient would look toward the corner of the room and smile. Sometimes they would begin speaking softly to someone who had already passed.

“I see my mother,” one man whispered peacefully.

Another woman reached out as if someone was standing beside her bed. “They came for me,” she said gently.

There was rarely fear in those moments. Instead, a deep calm would settle into the room like a soft light. The tension would ease. The atmosphere would shift. Even family members could feel it.

Something sacred was happening.

At first I didn’t try to explain these moments, I simply witnessed them.

But after sitting beside many people during their final days, a quiet understanding began to form within me.

The soul had never forgotten. It was the mind that forgot.

The soul carries its truth through every lifetime, quietly holding the memory of love, connection and the Divine. Yet the human mind, shaped by experiences, fears and the demands of daily life, sometimes loses sight of that deeper knowing.

And as the mind begins to loosen its grip at the end of life, something beautiful often happens.

The soul begins to shine through again.

I saw it in the eyes of people preparing to leave this world. Fear would soften. Peace would appear where worry had once lived. Love seemed to fill the room in a way that words cannot fully describe.

Those moments changed me. They taught me that death is not the disappearance of the soul. It is simply a transition where the soul begins to remember what it has always known.

Yet somewhere along the way I realized something even more miraculous...

The remembering was not only happening for the people I was sitting beside...

It was happening within me.

There were quiet moments in those homes, at bedsides surrounded by family photographs and the familiar pieces of a life someone had lived for decades. In those sacred pauses, the air in the room would grow still.

And in that stillness, something inside my own heart began to awaken. It was subtle at first. A deep sense of peace... a feeling of presence that seemed to fill the room. The same light I was witnessing in others was gently awakening within me as well.

My soul was remembering.

In many ways, those sacred moments at the bedside of people leaving this world prepared me for the work I now do with the living.

Years later I began to notice something just as miraculous. Remembering does not only happen at the end of life.

I began to see it happening in the people who came to sit with me in those sacred spaces. Not at the end of their lives, but in the middle of them.

People would arrive feeling lost, burdened or disconnected from themselves. Life had become heavy. The noise of the world and the weight of their experiences had caused them to forget something essential about who they truly were.

But when someone is given a safe and sacred space to pause, something begins to change. The mind grows quieter. The heart softens. And slowly, gently, the light of the soul begins to return.

I have seen it happen again and again.

I have watched people's eyes brighten as something deep within them begins to awaken. Not because I gave them something new, but because something ancient within them was remembered.

This is why I often say that my work is not about teaching people who they are; it is about helping them remember.

The soul never forgets its truth. Sometimes it simply needs someone willing to sit beside it long enough for that truth to rise to the surface again. Because remembering can happen at any time.

It can happen at the end of life, but it can also happen right now, in the middle of an ordinary day, when someone pauses long enough to hear the quiet whisper of their own soul.

And when that happens, something beautiful unfolds...

The light that was always there begins to shine again.

Calleen Russell - Soul Remembrance Guide, Energy Medicine Practitioner, and Sacred Sound Ceremonialist.

DivineWhispersByCalleen.com

https://www.facebook.com/calleen.russell

A Feng Shui Story: The Bagua Mirrors

Carmel Malone

About fifteen years ago, when I was first studying Feng Shui, we had very noisy neighbors living right beside us. The entire street complained about them. There were teens throwing stones at windows at three in the morning, cars with booming music and older teens riding bikes up and down the street late into the night.

No amount of talking with them made any difference. Every weekend the music was extremely loud. My children were younger at the time and needed their sleep for school. So I wondered what I could do.

I decided to place two Feng Shui Bagua mirrors on the side of our home facing the neighboring house. With these mirrors, the intention is always for the good of all involved. As I placed them, I set a clear intention: that the noise situation would resolve peacefully. I wished my neighbors well—good health, good work and good fortune in their lives.

About two months later, I mentioned to my Feng Shui teacher that the family with the teenagers had moved out of the house next door. She smiled and said,

"The Bagua mirrors worked." I thought to myself... indeed they did. With gratitude, I removed the mirrors and disposed of them.

New people moved into the house, and they were better neighbors. After about a year the music began again—not nearly as bad, but noticeable—so I placed the Bagua mirrors once more. Again, I wished everyone involved a healthy and prosperous life.
This time the neighbors were much more accommodating. They still played their music, but it was quieter and usually off by 10 p.m., which of course they are perfectly entitled to do. I left the mirrors in place.

Not long after, Superstorm Sandy, the largest Atlantic hurricane on record, hit the eastern seaboard of the United States. The storm was devastating across the region. Our home was spared. We only lost a few branches and our power was out for three days, while many around us were without electricity for one or even two weeks, and some had flooded homes. We were deeply grateful to have weathered the storm so well. About a week later, the Bagua mirrors fell off the house by themselves. I was astonished.

Fast forward fourteen years.

The house next door had fallen into serious disrepair. Squatters had moved in and one person appeared to be struggling with hard drugs. The owners were unable to maintain the property and eventually it was taken over by the bank. The police became a regular presence. So once again, I placed the Bagua mirrors.

And once again, I set the same intention: wishing good fortune, health and peace for everyone involved.

A few months later, the police evicted the squatters. I sincerely hope that those struggling with addiction found the help they needed.
That was about a year ago. The house now stands empty and in need of repair. I hope that one day someone will restore it and that a young family will move in and bring new life to the home. This time I have not been able to remove the

Bagua mirrors, so they remain there for now—perhaps for a reason I don't yet understand.

I also learned a lesson about how I approach neighbors; there is always a lesson for all of us in any life challenges if we choose to look for it. If I felt angry, I simply didn't go over to speak with them. Instead, I waited until I felt calm and could approach them in a pleasant way when asking them to turn the music down. This approach worked much better for everyone. It also taught me something deeper: when there is an issue in our lives, we are usually part of the situation in some way. When we change our energy or our approach, the situation often shifts too.

Note: Bagua mirrors are powerful Feng Shui remedies and should be used carefully. It is always best to consult a trained Feng Shui practitioner before placing them.

As a Feng Shui Specialist and a Board Certified Nurse Coach, I have spent years entering people's homes in different ways—sometimes through healthcare, sometimes through the lens of Feng Shui.

One pattern shows up again and again: most of us are living with far more than we need. Our homes slowly accumulate layers of excess. In Feng Shui, this excess can interrupt the natural flow of energy.

When we begin to remove these blocks, the change is often surprising. The home feels lighter, but so does life. Space appears. Time opens up. And with that space, people often find they can finally address what has been weighing on their health, their energy, and their lives.

Carmel Malone - Feng Shui Specialist and Board Certified Nurse Coach

https://createwithcarmel.com/

https://www.instagram.com/fengshui_everyday/

Love Beyond Borders: Finding Your Soul Mate After 40

Carol Davies

For much of my life, I believed that love stories belonged to the young—those who still moved through the world with unguarded hearts and skies that never frightened them. I had long admired them... the couples who laughed too loudly in cafés, the soft-eyed dreamers walking hand in hand under streetlamps. I had loved once, perhaps even twice, but each ending left quieter echoes, until my days became measured and methodical, like the ticking of a clock in an empty room.

At forty, my life unfolded in the rhythm of order and habit. The hush of the library where I worked became both my sanctuary and my solitude. I moved through the aisles as though among old friends with the scent of paper and dust and the weight of stories that never disappointed. Between ancient bindings and pristine new volumes, I found solace in other people's romances, in the tender illusions of fiction. I had convinced myself that the heart, once closed, could live meaningfully enough on imagination alone.

But life, ever unpredictable, has a quiet way of rewriting even the most careful of narratives.

It began without thunder or prophecy; just an international conference for librarians in Newark NJ in a mezzanine ballroom filled with badges, coffee cups and the low hum of professional chatter. The idea of "networking" seemed a polite euphemism for fatigue. And yet, there he was—standing by the registration table—his lanyard slightly crooked, his smile unstudied.

His name was Duncan and he was from Scotland. He was a librarian dealing with digital archives. We exchanged a few words about metadata, about the digitization of printed materials and then, as if guided by some quieter current, the conversation drifted into something else.

By the second day, I found myself searching for him in every corridor—his laugh, his thoughtful pauses, the way his eyes followed a speaker as though collecting meaning, not simply listening. There was an ease between us, an immediacy that defied our learned caution. I began to feel the slow ache of possibility—an emotion I had long believed to be extinct in me.

When the conference ended, parting felt abrupt, like being woken from a vivid dream. But Duncan wrote to me two days later...a simple message that began with a question about a paper I had presented and he ended with: *It felt good to meet someone who understands the silence between lines.*

And so, a bridge began to form across distance and across seas.

Our messages multiplied; first weekly, then daily. The professional pretext dissolved into something more intimate: long reflections on the lives we had led, the choices we had made and the things we still dared to hope for. We confessed our fears the way one might share secrets under the starlight. The correspondence became our communion—letters that crossed oceans as though distance was no more than paper and ink.

At night, I would sit by my window, eagerly reading his letters. They were tender, candid, sometimes imperfect, but they breathed life into my quiet existence. I could feel him there, within the sentences, in every hesitation of punctuation. Love began not as a thunderclap, but as the soft deepening of connection—a trust that grew through attentiveness and shared reverence for ordinary beauty.

When he finally arrived, months later, to visit in person, I saw him first through the blur of a crowd at the airport - that same unassuming grace, that same warmth that had traveled across thousands of miles through words. He smiled and I felt something inside me loosen, as if my soul had finally exhaled after years of holding its breath.

The week that followed was a quiet miracle. We wandered through museums and second-hand bookshops, lingering in the hushed corridors of the library where I worked. We cooked together, clumsy and content, laughing over spilled wine and overdone bread. At night we would sit in the living room, music whispering softly, our hands entwined on the couch. It wasn't the kind of love that consumes; it was the kind that awakens...delicate, steadfast, radiant with the ache of recognition.

There are moments I cannot quite name without diluting their magic - the way he looked at me when we talked, the way silence between us felt full rather than empty. In his presence, I learned that love need not rush or dazzle...it can arrive like the dawn, gentle but irreversible.

Our story, I think, is proof that love is a miracle. It does not obey calendars. It does not fade with age...it ripens. The heart, no matter how scarred, still remembers its way to wonder. To find him when I was forty was not some whimsical second chance; it was a homecoming. All those years of solitude had prepared me to recognize something rare and to hold it without fear, to honor it without haste.

Love, I have learned, is its own librarian gathering us, cataloging our humanity, preserving what might otherwise be lost. And in its careful keeping, two hearts, once separate and weathered by time, find their way to the same shelf still fragile, yes, but belonging, at last, to each other.

Carol Davies - Success Lifestyle Coach
https://thepassionmotivator.com
https://the passionmotivator.com/wp-content/uploads/2022/04/Born-to-Succeed.pdf

And I Rise Into My New Normal

Cheryl Kapitan

Writing for a book is a dream come true. So why, after years of writing daily, can I not move? Here I sit and it hits me... I didn't want this to be the time I begin and due to fear, fail to follow the project to the end. There are many stories in waiting... NDE, OBE's, Spirit messages and even a mind to mind chatter with a horse. Yet, this ordinary story, I bet, will hit home with many. Could completing this bucket list item be the miracle I could make my new normal?

So here it is: I sit at the start line, pen on paper; I rev my engine, anxious and keen. I rumble... now what?

I am a woman with many titles, most importantly and proudly, I am a single Mom. This is for all of those women out there who know this challenge and know this joy. As yours are too, my children are my everything. I chose to put myself aside, kept my word and raised my children to be strong. Both are now beautiful, kind, compassionate adults in their 30's. I wonder now who I am in the winter of my life. I sink into my chair, pen hovering... my eyes are drawn left by a movement in the window; it is the snow flying horizontally. How pretty, I think, that I am in here and it is out there and in the waves I wander. My gaze comes back to lines and ink. I want this writing to be interesting; I want this to help or even to inspire. I thought of a recent post I made where one ordinary day turned into an extraordinary day of rising. And here it is, my miracle is normal:

"Every day is a stunning reflection of our inner being, light filled or snow blown either way, always on a road less travelled."

My youngest child's summons was the startle I needed to get me out of my warm bed this morning. I forgot to set my alarm. Once up and simmered by a hot tea, I was ready to go. Then, like my slow rise, my car needed a boost. I usually call my eldest for such things. I looked up and saw his car 'Dahx' resting peacefully in the driveway and remembered that my son is on vacation. I called on 'Terrance' my youngest's car. He was vim and vinegar today but I had to speak softly to my 'Betty White'. "Betty, truly, I get it. Not an hour before, I felt your pain." I filled her windshield washer fluid, wiped her blades clean, hooked her up to 'Terrance' so he could give her a jolt. With a long, slow, grown, she coughed and then joined me on the day's crusade. A day of good work and still running, I took her to the trees and the stream; it was a beautiful day. Tonight, a blanket of snow keeps her warm.

Did I know how to boost my car by myself before this day? No. I have watched my son do it many times but never attempted it myself. My eldest being away, either I waited for his return or face the fear and do it anyway. Yes, the strong, seemingly confident Cheryl was afraid to boost her own car. Today my youngest and I were facing this thing head on. We watched a YouTube video; followed it step by step and in each move, bit by bit, the fear seemed to fade. In this tiny event was a beginning and I followed through to the end. I did it. We did it. My youngest and I with the cheers of texts from my son. In those tiny moments our family came together as one. I took a leap into the unknown and conquered a fear. With this gift, I am on my way to the next chapter of my life. In the leap, I took my power back. All the men who said without words, "you are woman, I am man", today, were being freed. In transition from the stigma, more independent, my self-awareness and my self-esteem rose. I drive proudly with my used jumper cables for the rare but possible chance I can help another single Mom sometime. More time to be brave, confident me. Because I am a woman, I had the power within me all along!

I began this write with enthusiasm, sat quietly in the magic of the middle and finally through fear I travelled and found myself proudly at the end. Two more things checked off my bucket list. Finding the miracles in the everyday and making them my new normal.

Cheryl Kapitan - Artist, Creative, Intuitive, Tai Chi & Qigong Practitioner & Distance Energy Communicator
https://www.instagram.com/cherylkapitan_art/
Cheryl.kapitan@gmail.com

Protected By Grace: My Journey Of Everyday Miracles

Cindy Edington

The explosion was so loud that it could be heard across the entire top floor of the building. I don't know how I walked away without a single scratch – it was undeniably a miracle.

At the time, I was working as an Associate Research Scientist for a pharmaceutical company. My focus was on the research and development of a vaccine for the influenza virus. That day, I had received a package containing frozen virus samples required for my experiments. Inside the package, there was a screw-top plastic container about the size of a quart of milk. The container held the vials of virus, surrounded by what appeared to be dry ice to maintain a frozen state.

I placed the container on the lab bench and began unscrewing the lid. Halfway through, I heard a strange vacuum-like hissing sound. Within seconds, the container exploded in my hands like a bomb. Thick shards of hard plastic shot through the air, whizzing past my face and neck.

Colleagues came running into the lab to find me trembling. A hole the size of a bowling ball gaped in the ceiling above me, and another one punctured the wall behind where I had been standing. Shards of plastic were scattered everywhere... on the lab bench, across the floor... Yet, somehow, I stood there completely unharmed.

Our health and hazard team was called to the scene, given the biohazard involved. Protocol required me to undress, go through a special cleansing process and put on a protective gown. They transported me to the hospital for a thorough examination. To everyone's amazement, I hadn't sustained a single injury. I walked out of the hospital with an overwhelming sense of gratitude and awe, thinking that this was truly a miracle of divine proportions.

This wasn't the first time Divine intervention had kept me safe.

I remember another moment vividly. I was sitting at a red light in the left lane of an intersection, waiting for the light to turn green. I had an inner feeling to look into my rearview mirror and I saw two cars speeding towards me, racing each other through the city. One of the cars veered off onto a side street, the other was heading straight for me.

Suddenly, I heard an unmistakable voice within me that said, "Move! Now!"

Without hesitation, I swerved into the right lane. A split second later, the speeding car screeched to a halt in the left lane where I had been moments before. Had I stayed in the left lane, the collision would have been catastrophic for both of us. The driver looked at me through his window and mouthed "thank you." I sat there in stunned silence, offering my thanks to God for the protection that had once again been granted to me.

These experiences are what I consider big miracles; moments where Divine intervention is so unmistakable that it takes your breath away. But I have also learned to recognize and celebrate the smaller everyday miracles that surround us.

Like when I get an intuitive nudge to reach out to a friend, only to discover that they were thinking of me too; or that they're having a tough day and needed someone to listen... or those moments when I ask the Universe for a parking spot close to the store on a rainy day and one opens up just as I arrive.

These little moments might seem insignificant to some, but I see them as gentle reminders of how connected we all are to the Divine. Miracles are everywhere when we choose to see them.

Over time, I have come to realize that the more I listen to my intuition, keep my heart open and ask for guidance from my angels, guides and the Universe, the more miracles I experience. It's as if the Universe is always waiting to show us its love-so long as we're willing to receive it!

I use several tools to stay connected to this Divine flow. Practicing gratitude, yoga, meditation, immersing myself in nature, journaling and Reiki are my go-to practices. Being part of a supportive community that recognizes the power of miracles helps to keep me grounded in this belief.

Ultimately, I have come to see that we are miracles. Each and every one of us. The simple fact that we're here, breathing, living and loving is miraculous in itself. And when we begin to view life this way, when we embrace the truth that miracles are normal, we open ourselves to a world filled with infinite possibilities.

How wonderful is that?

Cindy Edington - Author, Speaker, Transformational Life Coach, C-IAYT, RMT, EFT
https://tranquilheartwellness.com
cindy@tranquilheartwellness.com

Poetic Justice

Darylene Sherwood

I had been through many real-life traumatic situations before I turned 20 ... there was no such thing as counselling in those days. At 35 another real-life trauma struck unexpectedly. My husband tried to kill me ...

At the age of 21, I gave birth to a baby boy ... I was now a single mother. I couldn't find his dad. At 22 and out with friends one night, I met a tall and ever-so-charming male assisting at my friends' bar. Soon after that we started dating. He accepted my one-year-old and I as a package deal. We moved in together and lived happily until he did a runner. He returned months later. This happened four times. I was blindly in love so on his fifth return when he asked me to marry him – I said yes! In November his brother suddenly passed on. Family from near and far attended the wake. He thought we should get married then at the wake ... after all the family was there. We called an after-hours priest, got flowers and went back to the wake. A friend who had just returned from a fishing charter, in his bloody fishy gumboots, walked me down the aisle towards the priest and my future husband.

Happily married for 2 years my husband got a job outside South Africa's borders. We left South Africa in December 1999. I was going to be a housewife. In January 2000 I found out that I was pregnant and our child was born in September 2000.

A happy little family – life was great and he adopted my first son. After 2 years we relocated to another little town. Suddenly he went back to his old tricks and connected with a friend in Cape Town. He decided we would move back to Cape Town and get divorced.

Our neighbor's had a farewell dinner for us. My husband arrived drunk and rude; poured a glass of wine over our host and stormed out. I apologized and walked home. He then accused me of stealing his phone. I put my toddler to bed, went to the lounge and unzipped my high-heeled boots. I told him to go back and get his phone – it was not there. He started screaming at me and forcefully pushed me onto the couch; broke a beer bottle and started slicing my throat! When he saw the blood, he panicked and said he was sorry. He ran to get a towel. With unzipped boots I ran as fast as possible out of the back door, jumped over a meter-high wall and ran to my neighbor for help. The husband, tall and well built, ran to our house and grabbed my husband, held him up against the wall and had some real stern words with him. The police fetched me and took me home to sort out the issues. He had pushed the broken bottle under the couch and denied everything. I picked up my toddler, and the police took me back to my neighbor. The next day I was bruised all over my body and I went to lay a charge of attempted murder. He went to police station and paid an Admission of Guilt Fee of R100.00 (approximately $6.25c American). What an insult – my life was only worth R100.00!

The Magistrate locked the borders; demanding that he leave money for us. He did and minutes later he skipped the country. We were left behind and were now illegally in the country. His Company paid for us to get a flight back to Cape Town.

Back on home ground I rented a room, got the children into school and started work the following week. I got divorced in August 2004. He would now have to comply and pay maintenance. I tracked him down and summoned him. No maintenance was forthcoming.

I wrote to Interpol, People's Family Court, Foreign Affairs, Public Protector, Home Affairs, Constitutional Court, Human Rights Commission, National Prosecuting Authority, Peoples Family Law and many more ... nobody could assist.

He then fled to Canada where I had no address for him when out of the blue a parcel arrived from abroad with his address on the waybill. I felt hopeful and relieved, but to what extent? There is no justice in this country. Even worse was that I had to pay in money to collect the parcel. Very fulfilling though, as I now know his address. Feeling hopeful and with a new road to cross, I wondered if this could work? I was on a mission again but felt so alone. I knew I could not give up and I had to fight for my children's rights.

But the stress was too much!

I gave up.

One day I received a call from the Chief Prosecutor of the High Court asking if he could use me as a test case in the fight across borders for child maintenance.

I sent 75 pages of information to Canada. On the 2nd of February 2007, the first maintenance cheque for $320,00 arrived. My story was in local magazines and thereafter I helped many moms and dads with maintenance issues. I got three more maintenance cheques from Canada and then my ex fled to Mexico.

Lots happened over those years ... hard times and great times, health issues included ... but I am a proud mom of two amazing adult sons.

I look forward to sharing more stories of my life and helping people know that they are not alone!

Darylene Sherwood - Advocate For Maintenance After Divorce
https://www.facebook.com/groups/283013525182148/
https://www.facebook.com/darylene.sherwood

Coming Home To Myself Again

Debera Jensen

It was a beautiful spring day, really beautiful, with those gorgeous blue skies that you see in Colorado Springs, Colorado. I had left work at the Air Force Academy just a little early so I could go to an appointment. I was young, single and had landed a very prestigious job on the grounds of the Air Force Academy. I was very fit and I was having the time of my life, excited about building my new career and my life.

I was on my way to the appointment when it happened...the event that would change my life forever!

I was making a left turn and had looked in all directions. But at the last minute a car came roaring from behind a hill at a very fast speed. I couldn't possibly have seen him. He was out joyriding. Suddenly I realized that I was about to be hit and I couldn't escape the impact.

During those last minutes, my mind sped up and I was thinking of all the possibilities. I remembered seeing some headlines in newspapers about how the people that weren't going high speeds were the ones that were killed. I begged God to please help me to be able to see my father again, whom I loved dearly. I was so attached to him. That was about the last thing that I remembered.

I went to my doctor feeling so happy that I was alive! My immediate concern was that I may have broken my arm. It was heavily bruised and hurt a little. I asked him to check me thoroughly. Though I was badly bruised, he said that I was very lucky and that my arm was not broken.
I ended up going back to work pretty quickly because I had been told that nothing major was wrong.

Little did I know!

I remember walking around and being in shock pretty much the whole time. I was truly so happy to be alive!

My body didn't feel good, but I wasn't feeling all of the effects of the accident yet. It took a little while until I started to feel pain – a lot of pain. I couldn't think straight. I was really miserable.

My injuries started showing up. Strange things started happening. I was talking to a colleague one day in the hallway, just having a regular conversation. She said something to me; I know she did, but I couldn't understand it. It was as if she was speaking a different language.

I remember being frantic and excusing myself politely to go into my office for a moment, saying that I would be right back. I also remember literally praying when I was in my office because I didn't know what was happening.

I couldn't understand her and I was scared. I didn't know what to do. I went back into the hallway and greeted her once again and I was still praying inside of my head somewhere. She said something else. This time, miracle upon miracle, I could suddenly read lips and I understood what she was saying using the tool of lip-reading.

That was probably the second miracle.

By now even more of my injuries were showing themselves. I was starting to feel so much pain I could scarcely walk. I would go home and try to get comfortable but I could not lie down, or sit or stand comfortably. And obviously, I couldn't sleep.

The pain became excruciating. It was so bad and so unrelenting, I couldn't think properly. I was in such awful shape that I actually thought of committing suicide - and I don't believe in suicide.

I found some of the best doctors in the United States and they gave me all kinds of medicines for pain: muscle relaxants, lots of physical therapy, medicines, a TENs unit which was attached to my body and was supposed to cut pain but almost never did... maybe for a couple minutes.. twice...

I did chiropractic therapy, acupuncture .. you name it, I did it! Nothing worked.
I started to drink more... something I don't often do.
I even had some traction in the hospital, to no avail.

The doctors tried to cover all the bases but the pain, they said, was the worst that they had ever seen or recorded. Another problem with it was that it was unrelenting pain, it just never stopped. It was very debilitating.

I also found that I couldn't actually think like I could before. It just felt like my head was all fuzzy and unclear. And when I tried to find certain words, I just couldn't find them or it took a long time to find them; it felt as though there were large spaces between the words as I was trying to speak. I probably sounded fairly normal, but it didn't feel that way to me. I finally found a doctor who did a test and found that I had sustained a head injury. The head injury (now called a concussion), was the worst that they had ever seen.

As a child, I had been in accelerated classes and skipped grades in school. Now suddenly I was experiencing almost every learning disability you can think of - and probably more. I couldn't read properly, write properly or even talk easily anymore. My brain was having *mega* problems.

My doctors finally told me that my life as I had known it was over - at 28 years of age - and that I should accept it. That was hard to take! They said I had gone from age 28 to about age 80 or 85 years old in seconds... because of my injuries.

The doctors really couldn't help me...they did not have the answers.

I *had* to find the answers myself, because I knew I could not live like that much longer.

Two of those doctors probably saved my life. They came to me and said I should stop spending my money with them, because they did not have the answers. They wanted me to get better though, so they encouraged me to look into alternatives and then to come back and share the answers with them. I did not even know what an alternative was!

I searched... and searched... and even though I was told that the brain could not regenerate after a certain amount of time... or regenerate as much as we know now that it can, I *had* to find a way. It was survival – my survival!

I started taking classes ... in all kinds of energy work. I ended up taking classes everywhere, even in three different countries. Nothing could solve my problems although I got little inklings of possibilities; I finally had hope!

One of the first people I was sent to was a very well-known nutritionist who also did energy work. I don't think the nutrition helped much, but she recommended that I forgive the person who had hit me and to forgive God, whom I thought had let me down. I thought that was insane and I surely did not know how to do that nor did I want to do it! I was still really angry. She suggested I do it anyway...

Now I know that I needed to release the energy I was putting into hating the man and God...and bring back ALL my energy for healing purposes. She was right. Nowadays there are energy processes to help people to forgive.

I learned more and more about the brain and I found processes that would integrate and strengthen the parts of the brain that were still available to me and to strengthen the parts that had been injured.

And I found that the power of belief is amazing!

I was not given any hope by doctors, but...I met a man, Alan, who was very intuitive and he believed that I would come back from my injuries and be whole again. I thus had new hope (and he would later become my husband). What a gift he gave me!

I now know from experience that supporting beliefs can change anything and overcome what seems to be impossible! I also now know that negative beliefs can do the opposite. Nowadays science is beginning to prove that this is so as well.

I learned to release trauma. I learned so many energy tools that I can now teach to others. I learned that when you release trauma, many times the pain is released too.

Most of the doctors that I first talked to had not believed me. Only one doctor believed me. We had been friends who both happened to love music. He knew that I was healing. Eventually when the NFL concussion research was done, this friend was one of the major researchers proving that the brain could regenerate. The term for this is neuroplasticity.

A very big lesson I learned was that I was being led; I was following my intuition and finding the right classes. I was coming up with my own ideas. They call me an innovator but really, I think I was just being led. On the other hand, I did come up with solutions to many of my challenges. Then, a high profile doctor asked if I would help his patients.

Of course, I couldn't just leave people with no way out of their horrible injuries. If I could help, I would! And I knew I was coming out of my concussion - against all odds. My success was going against all the research I had done about the brain.

Looking back, I was guided every step of the way. Even though it was very hard and no one really knew how to come back from those types of injuries, I was Divinely Guided and I DID come back!

I have my life back!
I am no longer in pain!
I am so grateful!

The last picture of my spine (infrared imaging) made me nauseous. The doctors jumped back in horror and still say that I should be in immense pain. I am not in any pain at all. I work out 5 days a week; my body is quite agile.

I have loved ones and a business where I can now help others to come back from their pain and I teach people the energy/mindset tools that brought me back.

BIGGEST LESSONS?

I learned to question other people's beliefs about me, to trust my intuition and to know that my mind has immense power to change my body.

Debera Jensen - Health and Wellness Coach
https://www.wingsofheavenhealing.com/
https://www.facebook.com/debera.jensen

Inner Force Is Higher!

Debra C. Burton

"Today is the day you will die!" says the big rock I approach along the path on which I am walking.

I can't believe what I'm hearing! I turn around and look at the boulder. The rock repeats itself: **"Today is the day you will die!"** I shake my head, stunned, puzzled and in disbelief as I continue walking along the path.

When do miracles become normal?

...When the Inner Force Is Higher than any outside appearance.

Here is my story:

I am participating in a personal growth and spiritual development program out in nature to experience breaking through one's personal barriers.

On the path, I reach a cliff. There is a huge tree with a long line tied around it. That line extends over a deep valley to another cliff onto which the end of the line is tied to another tree. The man has me sign some indemnity papers to release them from any and all responsibility should anything happen to me and to affirm that I AM solely responsible. Then he tells me what I need to do.

"See that line over there?"

"Yes." I reply.

"You have to grasp the line between your hands and feet, and with your back parallel to the ground and your stomach facing up to the sky, pull yourself across the line to that cliff over there on the other side."

I only have a simple rope knotted around my waist and it is connected to the line I am supposed to traverse.

FEAR.

"Time for you to go!"

With trepidation, I firmly clasp the horizontal line between my hands and feet and I begin pulling myself across. As I get to the middle, I look into the sky and I think to myself: "Wow! The sky is so lovely!!! Such a clear blue sky! So vast! So beautiful!!!"

Hmmm, ... I wonder what it would be like, ... just to feel totally ...FREE?!?

Hmmm...I let go of the horizontal line with my hands...And then my feet...My arms and legs dangle below me like sticks.

I look down.

"OH MY! Look at those teeny tiny people!"

"And those trees are soooo small!"

I look up into the clear blue sky.

"WOW!" SO BEAUTIFUL! THE UNIVERSE AND THE CREATOR ARE SO VAST, SO WONDERFUL!!!

It feels so nice just to hang here FREELY! The single rope holding me is suspended at my waistline. My arms and legs are dangling below.

"It's sooo nice just to be FREE!"

From the other cliff, I hear the assistants calling me: "Come on, Debra!"

"Yes, yes! Just a moment!" It feels sooo nice just to hang here FREELY.

As I look down again, I realize: "Oh my, those trees really are quite tiny!"

I look into the clear blue sky: "How wonderful is THE PRECIOUS CREATOR, THE UNIVERSE!" So BEAUTIFUL!

"Debra!!! Come on!!!" shout the assistants.

"Yes, yes, I'm coming... just let me enjoy this a little bit longer...," I think to myself.

"Debra!!! We can't come and get you!!! PLEASE. COME NOW!!!" the assistants yell furiously.

"Okay, okay, ..." I think to myself: "It's so nice and freeing."

I attempt to raise my hands to clasp the line. But I CAN'T! No energy! The panic starts to build. I attempt to raise my feet to clasp the line.

I CAN'T! No energy! I CAN'T BREATHE! My lungs feel flat... like a sheet of paper. My body feels like an upside-down letter 'V' suspended at the top by the simple rope connected from my waist to the traverse line.

Now I know what the words meant that the rock spoke: **"Today is the day you will die!"**

"COME ON DEBRA!!! PLEASE!!! PLEASE!!! WE CAN'T COME AND GET YOU!!!

The assistants scream at the top of their voices, distraught and in full terror.

"OH MY GOODNESS GRACIOUS!!! I'M NOT READY TO DIE!!!"

The emotions well up almost to exploding in my body.

...I am crying ... and ... somehow... DON'T ASK ME HOW... SPIRIT tells me to breathe in the life-force energy from the terrified, panic-stricken assistants on the other cliff. I can literally SEE their life-force in their breath, something like an etheric, bubbly, yellowish, gaseous substance carrying their shouting words of desperation.

I B-R-E-A-T-H-E in the life-force from their breath... even though the assistants are so far away on the distant cliff.

I CAN BREATHE IN ENOUGH TO PULL UP MY ARMS, which have been hanging limp like overcooked wet noodles...

I CAN PULL UP MY LEGS!

I pull myself across, bit... by... bit... slowly inching my way to the screaming assistants. Reaching them with my last strength, they grab my body and yank it to the ground. They carry me down the mountainside on a stretcher. Now I understand the rock's REAL lesson:

Inner Force IS Higher! I AM DEEPLY GRATEFUL TO BE ALIVE.

Debra C. Burton, MBA, M.A.P - Self-Connection & Energy Faciliator, and Medium

Reconnexx.com

https://www.linkedin.com/in/debra-c-burton-144a89b/

The Miracle Of The Climb

Deston Rogers

"Sometimes you're stripped to your very soul in order to discover who you *really* are and what you're *really* made of. Only then can you start your climb back up."

I wrote those words because I have lived them. I know what it's like to lose *everything*. Well, not everything, but enough to bring a man to his knees.

How we handle adversity is the ultimate test of our character. Do we numb it with substances? Do we isolate ourselves? Or do we turn it over to God and lean into faith? Everyone handles their time in the dark differently. This is my story.

I am 59 years old. A father, a grandfather, a proud member of the Bishop Paiute Tribe and a man who has lived a dozen lifetimes. If you looked at my resume, your head would spin. I have worked alongside my father and brothers in construction. I have been in law enforcement across County, City, Tribal and International levels. I have served as Tribal Council Chairman, loaded sulfuric acid for gold mines (yeah, that was a dumb one), driven for Uber, managed nightclubs, served on submarines in the US Navy and spent over forty years in radio broadcasting. And... breathe!

I went to college for exactly one year. It wasn't my cup of tea—though the college women certainly were! I eventually found my footing in broadcasting school, where I was hired as an instructor the moment I graduated.

But the real story of my life isn't found in my job titles; it is found in the heartbreaks I have survived and the choices I have made. The truth is, I have made decisions that cost me relationships on all levels.

Along this chaotic journey, I have had the unbearable burden of burying two of my sons and their mother. My first son and his mom were taken in a horrific car accident. Crazy how trauma places a permanent timestamp on your soul. Thirty years later, his brother passed away at his job site due to alcohol. I nearly lost a third son to an ATV accident he wasn't expected to survive—but God always has the ultimate say.

Add to that the loss of both of my parents to a sudden tragedy and cancer, two divorces, bankruptcies and repossessions.

We so often walk around pretending everything is fine. But the facade that life is great is only a mask that sometimes hides the real, agonizing pain. Behind that mask, there were times when I seriously contemplated not being here anymore. That is the stark reality of my life. Put yourself in my shoes, and you would probably think the same thing. Actually, please don't put yourself in my shoes. You wouldn't want to walk in them.

So, where did I find the strength to get up for one more day?

That is where the miracle happened and continues to happen... I survived because of a loving family, true friends and an unshakable belief that God does not make mistakes. He has a purpose for me and knowing that I will one day be reunited with those I have lost brings a rejoicing to my spirit. Furthermore, I had to rely on a counselor to help me carry the weight - and I still do.

(If you are reading this and struggling, please don't be afraid to seek help. It is not shameful. It shows profound strength to admit you can't carry it alone. If you're in the US and contemplating something drastic, dial 988 right now.)

Speaking of true friends, I have learned the hard way that the community you build has a massive impact on the direction your life takes. They say you become the average of the five closest people with whom you surround yourself and I believe that down to my bones. My suggestion to anyone reading this? Choose your inner circle very carefully. Look at the people around you right now and ask yourself: Are they moving you closer to who you truly want to be, or are they a distraction keeping you stuck in the past? I'm not saying you have to cut people completely out of your life — we all have a history — but sometimes, creating a little distance is a very good, very necessary thing to protect your peace and your purpose.

If none of this heartbreak had happened, I wouldn't be who I am today. After four decades in radio, I realized that God had given me the gift of my voice for a reason. It took seven years of delays and divine timing to finally pull it together, but I eventually launched the *Eagle Freedom Presents podcast.*

My mission is to bring hope into a world where there is a void. I give people an avenue to share their journeys, proving that every single person has a story that can inspire someone else. Since launching in September 2025, the show has reached listeners in nearly thirty countries. Not bad for a guy from a small town in California!

My life is proof that miracles aren't just magical moments; sometimes, the miracle is the strength to keep going.

You too can Rise, Inspire and Overcome.

God Bless.

Deston Rogers Founder & Host, *Eagle Freedom Presents*

https://www.youtube.com/playlist?list=PLBx1_oW7-9fIgDj9-qK9y-AfRS_IlfnqO

https://www.facebook.com/eaglefreedompresents

Blessed By Fire

Dina H. Rose

I often say that I am in conversation with God. In truth, my whole life has been one long dialogue with the Divine.

This conversation began when I was three years old, after a tragic accident that changed the course of my life.

I was watching a bonfire when petrol splashed onto my dress and I caught fire. Suddenly everything was blazing, burning and excruciatingly painful. My father acted quickly, smothering the flames and saving my life. But during the journey to the hospital and the wait before I was treated, something deeper happened inside of me.

My parents were understandably terrified and in shock. As a three-year-old trying to make sense of the world, I interpreted their fear and concluded that I had no parents. Of course they loved me, I was their daughter, but from then on, I believed I could not rely on them as parents.

I had been told about God and I accepted Him as truth. In those moments I spoke to Him and I made a direct request: "Will You be my mother and father?"

And so, my conversation with God began.

The years that followed involved painful treatments and procedures. Looking back, I recognise that the trauma set me apart. Although outwardly happy and well-behaved, inside I felt like a guest in my parents' home, rather than a daughter who belonged. I tried not to cause trouble and I never answered back.

Instead, I became observant. I watched my parents, siblings and others around me. Without realising it, I learnt about human nature, behaviours and how emotions affect relationships. Each night I talked to God about my day, my life and my relationships.

Later our family went through a difficult period. As a child I couldn't understand what had happened, but everything changed. Our world collapsed and life became extremely challenging. There was very little money for basics such as fresh food. During those years I also experienced the heartbreaking loss of two baby brothers.

My parents, carrying enormous burdens, did the best they could under extreme circumstances. As children we felt the effects of these struggles without understanding them. Throughout those years I continued talking to God about my challenges, achievements and the deep loneliness I felt. In my heart I believed I was alone in this world, yet somehow, I also knew God was listening.

Life continued. I grew up, passed milestones and moved into adulthood.

In my twenties I experienced further trauma connected to family circumstances. Outwardly it appeared as if my life had fallen apart, yet my conversation with God remained constant. Until then, I was content with the one-sided communication. As I matured, my capacity for a reciprocal relationship expanded.

Then something interesting began to happen...God often seemed to respond.

I spoke, and life responded in ways that felt guided and personal. Seemingly impossible and amazing things started happening and became part of our ongoing dialogue. In my twenties I began marking the anniversary of the day I had been saved from the fire. Each year I paused to acknowledge the miracle and I shared the story with my children.

Then, thirty-one years after the accident, something really extraordinary happened...

I was alone in my kitchen on that anniversary, thanking God for saving my life all those years before, when suddenly everything fell into place. In an instant I saw the thread running through my life.

The burn had set me apart from my family. It led me, as a child, to turn towards God and to begin that lifelong conversation. Because of that connection, when my family later faced complex and painful circumstances, I was already standing outside of their dynamics.

What once felt like separation had become protection. What once felt like tragedy had opened a door.

As the realisation washed over me, I stood there in my kitchen with tears streaming down my face. In that moment I found myself thanking God, not only for saving my life but even for the accident itself.

What once seemed like the worst thing that could happen to a child had become, in ways I could never have imagined, an extraordinary kindness and miracle in my life. I understood something profound: sometimes the experiences that break us open are the very ones that guide us toward our purpose.

That awareness changed everything.

I began to understand how my experiences, the trauma, my observations and the constant conversation with the Divine, had been preparing me for the path I would later walk.

Over time I began helping others to explore their inner worlds, to understand their patterns and to gently heal the effects of trauma. Again and again, I saw how one person's healing created ripples far beyond their own life.

In hindsight, my life has always been guided through this ongoing dialogue with God. What began as a child's desperate plea for comfort, became a lifelong relationship. One long conversation with the Divine. And perhaps the most beautiful part is this: that conversation is open to every one of us, waiting patiently for when we choose to begin.

Dina H. Rose – Energy Therapist & Practitioner of Trauma Release & Emotional wellbeing
Dina.H.Rose26@proton.me

In The Midst Of Grief Miracles Do Emerge

Elaine Hale

When my daughter died, my life did not just change; it stopped making sense. The world did not slowly fade to black. It collapsed. One moment I was living the life I knew and the next I was standing in a reality I did not recognize. Nothing prepares a parent for outliving their child. It goes against nature, against logic, against everything a mother believes.

My daughter died on June 6, 2017, of a drug overdose. In the aftermath, time no longer worked the same. I was breathing, waking up, going through the motions, but I was not present. It felt like I was watching my life from the outside, disconnected from the world. Losing a child does not end when the funeral is over. It lives with you every day.

I started searching for the why. *Why her? Why opioids? Why could I not save her? Why love was not enough?* As her mother, the questions continued... they come in the middle of the night, in the quiet moments when the world has moved on and you are still standing in the wreckage.

I began to search for answers, needing to understand where she had gone and whether life continued beyond this world. I needed something or someone to tell me she was ok.

Grief does not arrive gently. It breaks you open. And in that breaking, something unexpected happened to me...

My spiritual awakening did not come wrapped in peace or understanding. It came through devastation. When everything familiar is stripped away, something deeper takes over. You become alert in a way you never were before. The distractions fall away, the ego sits quietly on the side lines. And whether you want it to or not, your soul begins to pay attention.

That's when I started noticing things: a song on the radio at the exact moment I was thinking of her; a feather appearing where it shouldn't; the feeling of her presence so strong it stopped me in my tracks. The signs came with timing too precise to ignore. They arrived when I needed comfort, not proof. They did not feel imagined. They felt known. There is a difference.

When a sign comes from the other side, it does not shout or demand belief. It settles into you quietly and brings a peace that makes no logical sense. It feels like love without words... like recognition... like something inside you, whispering, *"I'm still here."* Communication with our loved ones does not look like the movies. There are no voices booming from the sky. It's subtle, gentle and deeply personal. It comes through symbols, sensations, dreams and synchronicities. It comes through a sudden warmth, a memory that arrives unannounced, a knowing that does not need explanation.

I was panicking looking for a picture of my daughter for her obituary as I did not have many recent ones. I heard her voice telling me to calm down and go looking in her things and I would find what I needed. So, I took a breath and opened one of her boxes and there on top was the perfect picture... one that I had never seen before. I showed up at the funeral home and her father showed up with the exact same picture - we had been separated for many years. The only explanation for this is that she had chosen that picture herself and made sure we both chose it.

My daughter later came to me in a dream and she looked healthy. She was not struggling or suffering. She was simply herself. There she answered my question: she was okay and I was not to worry about her anymore.

Those moments did not erase my grief but they transformed it. Slowly, the question stopped being, *"Is she okay?"* I began to understand that death had not ended our relationship, instead it had changed the way it existed. She did not completely disappear. I knew she was still with me, just not in human form.

The greatest miracle I discovered was not that tragedy could be undone, but that love continues beyond it. I learned that love is not confined to a body; that consciousness does not end when we die; that our loved ones do not vanish, they transition, they remain aware, connected and capable of reaching us in ways we feel, before we understand.

When your heart is broken, when everything you thought you knew falls apart, the veil between us and the spirit world becomes thin. I did not consciously choose this path. No mother would, but it found me anyway.

Through one of the deepest losses of my life, miracles emerged and I discovered something undeniable:

Death does not have the final word.

Love does.

And love never dies!

Elaine Hale - Psychic Medium, Certified Clinical & Past Life Regression Hypnotherapist, Reiki Master
https://www.facebook.com/groups/1417137091969962

The Healer's Initiation

Erika Bernardini

Before the chakras, the crystals, the calm voice, the healer's hands...
there was a little girl who felt everything too deeply;
she was told she was too much for a world that didn't know how to hold her.

My journey into energetic self-mastery did not begin in a serene, healing room as some might believe. It began in the silence of childhood trauma, surrounded by abuse and heartbreak, in the shadows of wounds left unspoken. A consistent push to "fit in" to a world that I wasn't meant to be forced into. It began with the voices of those who claimed to love me while reminding me that I would never be enough; that I should shrink, tone it down and quiet the very essence of who I was. I grew up hiding my feelings like secrets. Tears were painfully punished, sensitivity was mocked, intuition intentionally ignored. Love always came with conditions - and safety was not my birthright, it was something I had to earn. I became a performer. The good girl, the helper, the one who never asked for too much.

But my inner child was always screaming for stability.
Screaming for softness. Screaming to be seen.

The wound was never a single moment but a thousand tiny cuts. From the emotionally absent adults abusing substances, to the chaotic environments I didn't belong in and the subtle shame of simply existing as I was, I learned to survive by disappearing into roles that were never mine. I learned to shape-shift to meet the needs of everyone but myself as survival, in a world where no one teaches you how to heal when you are still learning how to cope.

Those patterns followed me. They showed up in every adult relationship, every broken friendship, every trigger that sent me spiraling. I bent until I broke, then gathered the fragments in silence. To the world, I was smiling, strong, accomplished.

Behind closed doors, my soul whispered, "This isn't it." I didn't yet know that pain was an invitation. That the deep ache of unworthiness, of abandonment, of being both too much and not enough, would one day become the fire that purified me.

Before I became the healer, I had to be the wounded.□
Before I could hold space for others, I had to learn to hold myself.□
Before I navigated that initiation, I had to remember who I was before the world told me to forget.

On my 18th birthday in September of 2008, life really cracked me open. What should have been a celebration of freedom became a head-on collision. A near-fatal crash left me with a traumatic brain injury — with an invisible scar that would serve as both reminder and doorway. I remember waking in the aftermath, body broken but spirit vibrating with something unfamiliar. I was alive when I shouldn't have been - the knowing was immediate and undeniable: You are still here for a reason.

It was my first initiation. A symbolic death and rebirth and the beginning of my shamanic path, though I had no language for it then. Survival was no accident. It was a summons.

In the years that followed, I resisted the call. Life tested me again and again, pressing me against walls I thought would break me: failed relationships, financial strain, the quiet exhaustion of work and balance. Each trial was another whisper, "Are you ready yet? Will you remember who you are?"

Motherhood anchored me, giving me clarity and giving me a pure lesson in miracles. Love is the greatest protection and transformation begins in the home. Following a diagnosis of poly cystic ovarian syndrome, I was told I would never have children.

With each child I carried, I felt a deeper connection to something beyond myself. My womb wasn't just bringing forth life, it was birthing new layers of my own awakening.

Today, as I hold my sixth baby, I finally understand that my path is love and resilience and the reminder that miracles are not exceptions. They are normal, divine occurrences.

To the ones who thought I couldn't... or told me I shouldn't...
To the ones who tried to dim my light, who mistook my softness for weakness, who claimed to love me — but never learned how to love unconditionally...

To every "you'll never make it," every side-eye, every backhanded compliment, every room I was talked out of and every piece of myself I once gave away just to be accepted...

I leave it all here, between these pages.
This is the closure I never got; the healing I never knew I needed;
the truth I no longer apologize for.

May my light rise even higher because of the shadow I have walked through.
May these words make peace with every version of me I have ever been.
May no one ever again mistake my fire for something they can extinguish.

This is for me.
This is for the ones like me.
This is for the ones who believe in miracles.

Erika Bernardini - 200RYT Reiki Master Teacher, Wellness Coach, Fitness Instructor

https://linktr.ee/Erikabernardiniofficial

https://www.linkedin.com/in/erika-bernardini-5331a9b3

Taiga's Story

Fiona MacEachern

The room swirled in red, then green and then was obliterated altogether, so bright was the pure white light.

My throat tingled and sounds were flying around me.

My voice - powerful..

Gutteral...

Intense...

Low to high-pitched, pulsing and staccato. Energy was pouring, releasing, cold around me. My hands throbbed and so too, my ears.

A few feet away sat Taiga, my younger daughter, puzzle pieces clutched in each hand, intense blue eyes, a characteristic Mona Lisa smile etched enigmatically in bright red lips on her symmetrical face framed by golden curls.

She fluttered her jet-black eyelashes as a sudden surge of myoclonic seizures rippled through her body. Her brain was rebooting hundreds of times a day, leaving her scrambling to pick up the threads of her life every few seconds, making the playground swing terrifying and the gay abandon of whipping down a slide impossible. She would sometimes stagger or stumble if there was a particularly long episode.

Coupled with a sluggish digestion and circulatory system issues only diagnosed much later, she would later also suffer inexplicable episodes of 'heat stroke' during periods of moderate exercise in outdoor mild weather.

Taiga was known in three different departments in the Provincial Children's Hospital by the time she was 6, and four by the time she was 9. By the time she was 4 years of age, we had sought the advice of 27 health care practitioners to help with her health struggles and we had received few answers, been offered more tests and medications but no real solutions.

One heart-wrenching day, I realised it was up to me to help her.

So... in the words of Tracy Chapman, 'I quit school and that's what I did'.

I was on an academic track initially, a PhD (Zoology) and then pivoted to write for children, just finishing my second diploma when our world came tumbling down.

Taiga was diagnosed with three different types of epilepsy. After a series of ongoing vomiting episodes lasting up to 8 days and almost 3 dozen blood tests spanning about 3 years, she was eventually found to have Coeliac Disease. Switching immediately to a gluten-free diet, all new kitchen appliances to be dedicated gluten-free, did NOT actually stop the vomiting episodes, which lasted for another year, adding to the mystery. Genetic testing had found curious gaps - mystery DNA and the Western Medical world had given her another label by default.

By this time, I was a Reiki Master and had also been "activated" spontaneously to channel Light Language (calligraphy, hand signs and voice). I channeled daily as more signs and symbols poured through me. I wrote of my experiences, experimenting and sharing them in smaller circles. I could feel the power as it channeled and swept a broad path in my central channel through me. It cleared and it brought universal truths from the Akasha.

"It shifts DNA", I learned.
"It toggles epigenetics and makes change at the cellular level, the most powerful healing energy on the planet."

When I feel confident about my abilities, I will work on Taiga, I told myself one day. After a particularly trying day, with tummy troubles, tantrums and triggers, I approached a then-colleague for a co-session for Taiga.

The anti-seizure medications that Taiga was eventually prescribed, after an unhappy trial and error period of 2 or 3 other drug types, dated from the 1950's and caused severe aggressive behaviour, constipation and drowsiness. They also had to be administered exactly 12 hours apart or run the risk of another seizure. And Taiga's heart rate already ran high.

"Let's do Light Language and wean her off these drugs," I said.
"Let's do it." was the response.

A week later I was sitting before a series of Light Language symbols drawn on cards. The room buzzed with electricity, powerful sounds and fields of light energy for about 10 minutes and Taiga giggled and waved her chubby hands every time she placed a puzzle-piece. Speech was not easy for her and we spent years patiently encouraging her to expand her short phrase conversation exchanges with us.

As the energy eased and softened and the swirling reduced to gentle waves, it was like the spell was broken. She rose, bum first, as she put the puzzle pieces down – she only had a few left to put in place - and turned and raced from the room, calling the cat, "Pennyyyyyy!".

A few weeks later we were back at the hospital for Taiga to have another EEG, and we received the amazing news that her scan was pronounced "clear". It was time to wean her off the drugs. A few days later, while helping her to wash her long, curly, golden hair, I looked at her toes and my heart began pounding. All her toenails had horizontal lines running through them. Above, the toes were thick and malformed, below the line they were perfect, and her toes were straighter. The time period corresponded exactly to the day of the healing session.

The DNA healing was borne out in her toenails as an unpredicted side-effect of the Light Language healing.

I believe in Miracles!

Taiga also never had another vomiting episode again.

After that, I knew I had to share this Divine gift with others. Light Language works powerfully and multidimensionally to clear energy and deep emotional blocks, often in the container of a Forensic Healing™ session.

Fiona MacEachern - Purpose Catalyst Coach and Energy Alchemist for mature women
https://mossomcreekwellness.com
https://www.facebook.com/profile.php?id=100063714543098

The Miracle Of Argan

Germaine Vogel

The sheer presence of Argan struck me when he first arrived at my Kyalami stable yard in 2015.

As he lowered his majestic head into my open palms, I felt his inquisitive warmth drawing me in, his velvet muzzle inviting a quiet, deliberate connection, a familiar silent exchange between two worlds....a meeting of souls. I gazed into his calm, gentle eyes and my heart sensed his acceptance. "I know you," he seemed to be saying....a proud prince, liquid gold in the sunlight.

Had we met before?

I had actually heard about Argan some years previously. Living in KwaZulu-Natal, my stable-yard partner would return from Johannesburg, enthusing about a magnificent horse whose overseas owner flew in just to compete in top dressage shows. How extraordinary! "Honestly Germaine, you wouldn't believe the size of him - 18 hands - and so gentle, so intelligent... I'd give anything to own that horse."

"I'm not really into the competitive side of the horse-world," I replied indifferently, thinking of leisurely hours spent cantering through rippling sugar cane fields with friends, riding endless green paths leading to beaches where we waded with our horses in the warm waters of the Indian Ocean.

In 2014, I found myself living in Nairobi. I had flown my three South African horses out to Kenya with me, as I could not bear to sever our deep, unspoken bonds. My first Kenyan outride took us through the Dagoretti Forest in Karen. Trotting along cool tree-lined paths shared with Maasai herdsmen, cattle, and athletes in training, I was surprised to learn that my fellow rider, the owner of the yard where my horses were stabled, was leaving the following day for Johannesburg to enter a horse she kept there in a prestigious show.

"Is your horse called Argan?" I asked out of the blue. "Yes," she replied, a little surprised. "How did you know?"

"NO!!! I can't believe the coincidence. My stable partner in Umdloti is always going on about how amazing he is." I raised my voice to match hers over the sound of drumming hooves. Here I was, in equestrian heaven, with the woman who owned the big brown horse of which I had heard so much.

She continued to regale me with Argan's story, explaining how she had acquired him in Rwanda and transported him to Johannesburg. "He is a brilliant horse," she said affectionately, "but I need him to compete in South Africa. We just don't have the same international dressage standard here in Kenya yet."

Argan was born in rural Quebec in April 2005 and laid to rest in Cape Town in December 2023. At three years old, his Canadian breeder moved with him to Kigali, Rwanda, to join her sister. You could say Argan's life story was shaped by the ripple effects of history; by Canada's response to the Tutsi genocide of 1994, which had evacuated Rwandan children to safety. Love eventually brought one evacuee and his Canadian family back to verdant Kigali.

Not long after arriving in Kigali, Argan's breeder returned to Canada, selling her two stallions to the woman I had met in Nairobi. She had him gelded and packed him off to South Africa to showcase his considerable talents in the competitive arena. His new owner and I became close friends. We shared adventurous days exploring her upmarket world of semi-rural Karen. After mornings spent with the horses, we would make our way to cosy cafes, followed by refreshing swims at the Country Club. Another favourite amble of ours was vintage shopping at the friendly local markets in Kibera, arguably the largest informal settlement in Africa. We enjoyed art and music fairs and attended many of the Nairobi social events on offer.

My husband and I were fond of our Nairobi house with its immense, lush garden and serene view stretching all the way to the Ngong Hills. We enjoyed early evening walks with our dogs through the peaceful neighbourhood. When our children and friends visited from South Africa, we would proudly take them to the world-renowned elephant and giraffe sanctuaries nearby. I had settled into a vibrant routine, thinking that this was how life was going to be for the next five years.

Then one evening, my husband dropped a bombshell..."What do you mean, your contract has ended?" I couldn't breathe. "We need to leave as soon as we can," he replied, devastated. "No, there are no direct flights back for the horses!" I wailed.

I had flown my horses to Nairobi, not foreseeing that by the end of that same year I would be trucking my precious companions back home through Kenya, Tanzania, Zambia and into Zimbabwe. It was an arduous five-day journey fraught with dread, fear, hunger and discomfort. By the time I reached Harare, I was humbled by the kindness, gratitude and forgiveness I found on those pot-holed roads. I gained insight into the adversity Argan must have endured, being transported from Rwanda, and then on that same route to South Africa.

By February 2015, my horses and I were living in Kyalami. Argan's owner came from Nairobi to stay with us when competing in a show and decided to move him to our yard. That is how I met Argan and I finally understood the adulation for him that I had heard about over the years. I was in awe.

Then came another miraculous meeting. His breeder had believed she would never see Argan again. In 2016, she reunited with him in my yard! It was an ecstatic moment. She had flown from Canada to assist her sister, who had been brought from Kigali to Johannesburg for emergency hospital care.

Through the fortunate connection with Argan's owner, I was able to accommodate all of us. Resting in sunshine, surrounded by the quiet healing presence of horses, our gravely ill patient's health gradually returned. It was remarkable how all of us strangers were drawn together through uninvited events. I could not know then that Argan would one day be mine. Looking back, I realise we were possibly a gathering of his chosen carers.

Argan's breeder had known at his birth that he was a rare gift. "Don't miss the opportunity to have a foal from him", she suggested, packing her suitcase. "I think a foal from Red..." "You know, funny you say that....an animal communicator recently told me that Red yearned for a foal" I interrupted as we smiled at each other.

I was heartbroken when Argan was put up for auction in 2017 and moved to another yard. "I'm so sorry", I said to him the day he left. There was nothing I could do and I worried about what his future held. It wasn't long before his new owners appointed a skilled young rider to compete him. As fate would have it, she lived in one of the cottages on our property and I got to hear all his news and to attend his events.

Two years passed when I got a frantic call from his young rider: Argan had been severely injured. Tearfully, she explained that he would be mechanically lame and no longer sound for competition and that the obvious choice was to euthanize. "Do you want him?" she asked, weeping... "It's the only other option...He won't pass vet tests and he can't be sold... you will only be able to walk on him....he can't carry any heavy weight... he might go permanently lame, so you would eventually have to make the decision..."

Life with Argan unfolded into a treasury of sweet memories. When he stood tall, ears forward, his great whale-bone frame towering beside me, I would rest my hand on his shoulder so he knew I was there. My first ride on him was through the open veldt and forests that surrounded our house. We only had a few months in Kyalami as my husband and I were readying to move to Cape Town at the end of 2019.

Argan moved with us and, once settled, we found new riding paths through leafy suburbia, across a river into the fynbos of Table Mountain, overlooking the beauty of the Atlantic Ocean.

I remember one cherished moment: mounting in my arena, preparing for a gentle ride to the river, how he softly gathered himself into dressage form and cantered figure-of-eights with flying changes. I didn't stop him. It was a gift. He knew far more of the art of riding than I did, and this was his way of sharing it. With his enormous, floating strides I felt the earth sing each time his hooves landed.

I would lie beside him while he slept, his breath warm on my cheeks. He had a deep lion-like purr, as though his heart itself was strumming happiness. He would come into our house whenever he could, enormous and perfectly still, filling the entrance hall yet never breaking a thing. Sometimes he slept standing on the veranda, his breath misting the glass so that he appeared ghostlike from inside.

Ruby-Moon, Argan and Red's daughter was born in 2021.

We didn't get to spend the rest of our lives with Argan but he got to spend the rest of his life with us, in retirement, free from all expectations.

In 2023, Argan's health took a turn for the worse and we had to make an agonising choice. Through his pain, he wordlessly communicated that his great soul was ready to leave. After the vet had been, Ruby and Red stood watch in silence over his peaceful body, lying in an open field, as if in a prayer to the earth.

The spirit of Argan lives on in his daughter, for Ruby-Moon embodies her father's dignity and sweetness, coupled with her mother's intuition.

She calls to me with Argan's same quiet purr. Not yet fully grown, but already standing tall and proud, her heritage spans eons and continents. Ruby-Moon truly is our miracle child.

Germaine Vogel - Equine Facilitator
https://www.instagram.com/taming_maine
https://www.facebook.com/germaine.vogel.9

Everyday Miracle: Scully

Jacky Foss

On 12.06.2007 a miracle entered my energetic field. It wasn't until three months later that this same miracle entered my heart.

The miracle arrived in the form of my fur baby, Scully, a gift from heaven wrapped in stubborn devotion and four small legs.

Scully was the most precious gift I received. She had the strength of an ox, the attitude of an ascended master and the heart of multiple universes. Throughout her eighteen years, Scully pushed and smashed through boundaries, exhausting our patience while contributing generously to the already heightened anxieties of our family unit.

Scully took up space, controlled the narrative and restricted our movements. In doing so, she forced me to confront my own inner demons, my resistance to expansion and to explore my own fear of growth. I didn't know it then, but Scully wasn't just living alongside me, she was shaping me.

We used to come home in our lunch hour to let her out to piddle as she couldn't be left outside alone, due to her separation anxiety which contributed to behaviors we didn't yet understand. Scully smashed through three windows two millimeters thick and hit the ground running, crossing multiple lanes of traffic, just to find me. I used to think that this was something to manage, to fix. I see now that it was something to honor.

Scully was teaching me that love does not tolerate absence; that connection is not theoretical; that devotion is a lived act and not a feeling.

Through it all Scully didn't' want freedom from me, she wanted freedom *with* me.

We agonized over bringing Scully back home to New Zealand as we didn't want to put her through the flight, the containment, the unknown of what laid ahead for all of us. We imagined that the trauma would be too much for her. In the end it was us who were more traumatized by the thought of leaving her behind. So we brought her home and it was as if her body recognized the land before her mind could catch up. Scully ran differently, breathed differently and loved differently.

Scully got to experience my homeland, the air that raised me, the soil that shaped me, the wide spaces that held me without asking questions. I watched her become more herself here and in doing so I remembered something I had forgotten:

Belonging isn't about ease, it is about remembering.

The choice to bring her home despite the fear, was another everyday miracle. Not loud, not celebrated, just a quiet yes to love again.

In her final months, Scully's body began to slow down in ways that were impossible to ignore. The strength that once carried her through windows and traffic softened into something quieter, something more deliberate.

I began to listen differently; I watched more closely, learning the language of small changes. Love became less about doing and more about noticing, staying close and making space for all the emotions to land.

Choosing Motherhood

I always said I never wanted to be a mother and to have kids as I felt I would have needed to give them everything. Only recently did I realize that I was a mother and that I did give everything. Just because I chose to be a mother to a canine and not to a human doesn't change anything. I gave my girl everything: unconditional love, limitless compassion and kindness while allowing her space to grow and explore. 9 times out of 10 she explored by herself as she was an escape artist who would wander surrounding neighborhoods.

The space that was taken up by her provided us room to step into a reality of trust, sacrifice and discipline; only now that she has left our home at the age of 18, we find ourselves in a new predicament. We are having to navigate the silences hanging in every room; no more interrupted nights and the endless possibilities of freedom.

Our voices are being heard.
No more being submissive.
We thank our baby girl for holding space so that we could experience love.

Now it's our time to let go...
To Honor her, to respect her final wishes.

Together we walk our paths of enlightenment and faith, trusting, knowing we will meet again. There was a moment when I saw Scully's body soften and her breath change. No fear, no struggle, just resignation. Her time here was complete. I stayed with her, not to hold her back but to let her know she was free to go.

In the weeks that followed, I felt her presence everywhere... in pauses, in habits, in the places my hand still reached without thinking. I began to understand that some miracles don't end, they just change form.

Scully was my everyday miracle, not because she stayed but because she taught me how to love without distance and how to release it without breaking.

And that miracle continues...

Jacky Foss - Poet - The Art of Remembering
www.jackyfoss.com
jackyfoss01@gmail.com

Walk The Perimeter

Jacqueline Gale

Fourteen years ago, the day began with urgency in every direction. It was the morning of the impending "Hurricane Sandy". The storm was approaching faster than anyone expected and the island was alive with motion. As we prepared to evacuate our island home, I had a sudden 'prompting', but in the frenzy of preparing to leave, I ignored it. Police cruisers rolled slowly down each street, loudspeakers commanding immediate evacuation. I hurried through the house gathering what little of our earthly treasures could fit into a car — photographs, family keepsakes, the irreplaceable fragments of a life. I drove my mother off the island to stay with trusted friends where she would be safe and then returned to finish securing our house. Windows were taped. Patio furniture was tied down. Anything that might take flight in the coming winds was put away. The entire morning carried a sense of urgency that pressed against every moment.

Yet something about those days felt different long before the storm even arrived. For nearly two days the air itself felt strange. The barometric pressure had dropped so sharply that our ears popped as though we were climbing in an airplane. Headaches lingered. Sinuses ached. The atmosphere felt heavy and unsettled. On the morning of the evacuation, I stood at the end of the street and looked towards the bay...what I saw stopped me. The water appeared higher than the road itself, as though the bay had risen above the land. I stared, trying to make sense of it, wondering if the strange pressure was somehow holding the water unnaturally high. Something was wrong, though I could not yet name it.

Until then, most storms we had known typically came from the ocean side. Flooding would push in from the beach and run down the streets toward the bay. But this time something entirely different was unfolding. As the storm intensified, the rising tides in the bay resulted from a bridge collapse further north, miles away, unleashing a rushing wall of water that surged southward in the back bays and mainland shorelines. Water now pressed in from both directions — bay and ocean. The island would soon be overtaken in a way no one had ever experienced before.

And it was in the midst of this urgency, with evacuation underway and the storm only hours away, that the 'prompting' returned a second time with such clarity that I knew I could no longer ignore it. This time the voice was unmistakable... clear, direct and strong enough that it stopped me in the middle of what I was doing. I suddenly became aware that the thought had not come from my own mind. There was an authority in it that was impossible to ignore. I still did not understand what it meant or why I would be asked to do such a thing, but the urgency in the instruction demanded a response. This time I listened and acted.

"Walk the perimeter."

The first time I heard the instruction, I dismissed it immediately. It seemed like such a strange thought that I brushed it aside as nothing more than my own imagination. In the middle of preparing for evacuation, with police urging residents to leave and the storm only hours away, the idea felt almost absurd. I had too many things to do. There was no time to entertain thoughts that made no sense.

But I stepped outside.

The air felt heavy and strange, thick with the pressure that had lingered for days. The wind was only a light breeze, although the tide had already begun its quiet advance. In just a few hours the water had crept nearly halfway from the water's edge towards the dune. The sea was rising, though the full force of the storm had not yet arrived.

I began to walk.

Step by step I followed the boundary of the property, tracing a path I could not have explained, yet somehow understood. I walked along the edges, across the sand near the dune line, turning where I felt led, continuing until the path brought me back toward where I had started. I had traversed a large square, praying as I went.

At the time, I did not know why I was doing this.

I simply obeyed. I didn't understand the ramifications that this would have at the time, but looking back, the results of my obedience to the call were Miraculous.

I have always believed that when we carry the Spirit of God within these earthen vessels, even our footsteps become Holy when we walk in obedience. That day, though I did not yet fully understand it, I sensed that my steps mattered.

The sand shifted softly beneath my feet with each step, warm and unsteady, as though even the ground was aware that something was coming. The air was strangely still, carrying a quiet weight that pressed in around me. With each step, I became more aware that this was not something I was simply choosing to do — I was being led.

When I returned to the place where I had begun, I stopped.

Even now I struggle to find words for what I felt in that moment. All I can say with certainty is that I believe with all my heart that it was God Himself who led me, telling me where to walk, where to turn, how far to go and ultimately guiding me back to the place where I began my walk.

I looked around and I took it all in.

This had been my home for more than fifty years. My childhood dwelling, the place where so many memories had been made. I found myself speaking quietly to God, thanking Him for all the wonderful years I had spent there, for the life that I had enjoyed in that place and for the neighbors who had shared that community with me.

I asked Him to have mercy on us all, not just for our homes, but for every family, every life and every unknown outcome that lay ahead.

Gratitude filled my heart in that moment. I have always believed that gratitude begets more gratitude and standing there on that dune I felt a deep peace settle over me. Whatever was about to come, I placed in His hands.

My part had been to listen and to walk.

When that moment passed, I returned inside, finished packing what little we could carry and prepared to leave. Within a short time, I would drive away from the home I had known for more than five decades, uncertain of what would remain when the storm had passed.

The storm came with a force that few had imagined.

Gas lines failed. Water lines broke. Electricity disappeared. The island became a dark zone. For nearly three weeks no one was permitted to return. Reports of looting circulated and the National Guard stood watch at checkpoints, allowing no one through.

When we were finally allowed back, it was only to survey the damage. Utilities were still out and no one was permitted to remain overnight.

Driving toward the island that day, my heart was heavy with uncertainty. After everything we had heard...the flooding, the destruction...I prepared myself for the possibility that little might remain.

When I turned onto my street, I could hardly believe what I was seeing. There was sand everywhere, piled high across the road as though the ocean itself had rolled through and then retreated. Some roofs showed minor damage. A few oceanfront homes had broken windows and shattered sliding glass doors.

But something else immediately caught my attention.
There was no flooding.
Not on our street; not within the perimeter.

I stood there, trying to comprehend what I was seeing. All around the island, we had heard of water pouring through homes, four and five feet deep in places that had never flooded before. Entire neighborhoods and businesses had been devastated.

Yet here, within this small stretch of homes, the properties were virtually untouched. Only when I drove farther down to the street did the full contrast become apparent. Beyond that point, where the homes ended and the businesses began, the water had surged in from the bay side.

The difference was staggering.

One side was ravaged by water. The other side had been spared; literally along the perimeter where I had walked that morning... everything had been protected.

A neighbor who had remained on the island during the storm later told me that she was terrified having never experienced winds or flooding like that ever before. At one point, it became too dangerous to leave and so she was forced to stay. That night the wind howled relentlessly as the water surged through the streets.

After the worst of the storm had passed and the waters began to recede, she ventured outside. Her yard was flooded, and the surrounding streets were still covered in water and debris. But as she proceeded up our street, she noticed something remarkable: The flooding had simply stopped.

Where the water had filled yards and the streets nearby, the homes within that small stretch were dry. Sand had been pushed across the road, but the houses themselves had been spared.

She walked to my home and seeing that I had evacuated, took a photograph so that I could see what remained.

I was speechless.

There was virtually no evidence of flooding at all; only a few roof shingles lying in the yard.

Our street had been spared. As I walked up to the dune, there was now a 15-foot shear drop across the dune exactly where I had walked. When I saw it, I was stunned. It was miraculous. This was truly a moment when the miraculous became undeniable.

People may consider it an odd circumstance of the storm — one street untouched while others were not. Few ever knew why that particular stretch of land remained protected, while everything around it was ravaged.

I never felt the need to explain it, but sometimes we are asked to act in ways that seem small or even strange and we may never know why, but the impact is real.

Miracles are often quiet acts of obedience whose impact may not be fully known. Sometimes God asks us to act before we understand. And sometimes the miracle lies not in the voice itself, but in the simple willingness to listen and to walk where we are led.

Fourteen years later, I still carry the quiet certainty that those steps mattered.

This is a miracle I will cherish all my days. I share it not for recognition, but as a testimony that God is alive; that He still speaks, still leads and still moves on behalf of those who are willing to listen and to act.

"He speaks and the waves are stilled. He calms a storm by commanding the wind and waves to be silent." (Psalm 107:29-31)

What once felt like an extraordinary moment has, over time, revealed a deeper truth to me: that the miraculous is often found in the quiet places, in simple acts of trust and obedience. And in that understanding, I have come to see that miracles are not distant or rare events reserved for a few.

Miracles are, in fact, Normal for all.

Jacqueline Gale - Transformational Retirement Life Coach & Travelpreneur
https://www.facebook.com/jackie.gale.144
https://www.linkedin.com/in/jackiegalenewlifenow/

The Death Of Me Was A Blessing For Me

Jacqueline Zralka

In all of His glory, standing right in front of me, there He was. I stared at His feet as I felt so overcome by the presence. I could not bear the emotions I felt from the bright, warm light radiating from Him. All I was able to do was cry uncontrollably, not out of sadness, but from the feeling of pure unconditional love. His company alone made me feel as though everything would be okay and that I did not have to worry about a thing. He loved me and saw me for exactly who I was. His beautiful, long, curly hair lay perfectly on the long white robe that draped over His body. He looked exactly how I had always imagined. Meeting Jesus himself was something I had always dreamed of since I was a little girl. I thought I would only get to meet him once I passed away. Then suddenly, my feeling of excitement and warmth turned slightly to sadness and disappointment. *Does this mean I am dead? Am I in heaven?*

My near-death experience came out of nowhere. I was fine one day and sick in the ICU the next. The first trip to the doctor was quick: a simple diagnosis of a UTI, a prescription of antibiotics and back home to rest. The second trip was to the emergency room and it turned into something from a nightmare, something I was not sure I would make it out of. The day started like any normal day except that I had woken up with a slight headache, but nothing some Tylenol couldn't fix - or so I thought. We had plans to go to my sister's house for a Memorial Day barbecue. It was very warm outside that late May day, but I could not get warm. My husband noticed me shaking and asked if I was okay. I brushed it off and said I was fine, as I usually do when something doesn't feel right. I just hated hospitals and avoided them like the plague.

In the car on the way to my sister's house, my body was shaking uncontrollably. The inside of my body felt like ice. And, to add to the chills, my headache was worsening to the point where I had to wear sunglasses and keep my hands over my eyes to block out the sunlight. I felt terrible for my family as they were basically forced to be in a sauna for the entire drive, but they dealt with it and I knew they were worried. Once we got to our destination, my family begged me to go to the hospital because clearly, something was not right. I, of course, refused for as long as I could, but eventually I caved. Deep down, I agreed: something was not right. Surprisingly, I was rushed into a room and doctors started running tests immediately. Tests found that there was an infection in my bloodstream, later known to have been caused by my UTI. My body was in septic shock.

The next few days in the ICU felt like a long, traumatic, fever dream. I was repeatedly probed and prodded whilst slipping in and out of consciousness. Doctors even quarantined me in case the infection was caused by meningitis, which thankfully, a spinal tap ruled out. My kidneys were failing as I still had no output by day three. Doctors pumped me with fluids and antibiotics in the hopes that I would urinate and beat this infection, but time was running out as nothing was helping my case. Eventually, they brought in the CDC for what I assume was the last resort. *They flew in the CDC just for me? Am I that important?*

By the third morning, I was completely out of it. My family later told me I was totally out of sorts and saying things I would not normally say. This infection was altering my personality, making me unrecognizable to my family and friends. I remember sitting up in my bed, or trying to at least, and seeing about 5 doctors just staring at me with a bewildered look on their faces. At this point, I was angry. I was shivering uncontrollably and in excruciating pain from a headache that made my head feel like it would implode from the pressure. All this pain was caused from this infection that had depleted my body of any comforts, this infection that these doctors had failed to heal me from. I started spewing words at them uncontrollably, like word-vomit. "Don't just stand there! Help me, you morons!" I couldn't contain myself or the words coming out of my mouth. Except that no words were coming out of my mouth and I was not sitting up in my bed like I thought I was. I realized that I was not in my body anymore. The room slowly darkened until everything was black and the sound of the hospital room echoed out. Everything was silent. My pain was gone and an overwhelming feeling of warmth came over me.

I then heard a calm female voice say, "It is time to come with us." I saw three life-sized feminine silhouettes of pure, golden light. They took my hands and we started walking. The environment turned bright and warm and we were in a beautiful, golden field. I cannot express the joy and excitement I felt at being in their presence. Everything about this place and these beings felt like what you would expect the energy of the sun to feel. They led me to the tree line where we walked through the most beautiful forest. Tall trees dancing in a warm breeze full of life. Ground blanketed in bright, colorful flowers you could probably see for miles. I began to hear the sounds of a waterfall getting louder and louder with each step. The most joyous, genuine smile had not left my face since joining hands with these beings. *This is so cool!* We eventually got to the other side of the tree line that revealed the most amazing sight I had ever witnessed in my entire life. The waterfall dropped into a vibrant, turquoise lagoon surrounded by magnificent greenery. The scene looked like something out of a Disney movie. One of the golden beings turned me away from the waterfall and gently let go of my hand. She said, "Wait here." They walked behind me but I stayed still. *What was I waiting for?* I wanted nothing more in that moment than to look at the waterfall again. The vibrancy and beauty were unmatched by anything I had ever experienced. I craved the sight of it. My anticipation got the best of me and I turned around to get one more look while I was waiting for who knows what.

When I turned around, there He was.

We talked for what seemed like several hours, telepathically. Although I do not remember what was said, I know that at the time, it needed to be heard by her, my old self. He laid his hand on my head multiple times and words will never be able to describe the feeling. A father figure of overwhelming love and acceptance is the closest way I can try to explain His aura. I do remember one thing He asked me though, and it forever changed my perception of life. He asked, "Do you want to stay here?" My face lit up with an ear-to-ear smile and I nodded my head vigorously. *I want nothing more than to stay here forever!* He then tapped His foot and the ground turned to glass. I looked down and my smile faded completely. I saw my family, my husband and my two daughters in the hospital room crying and praying. I started to panic and shook my head. *I can't leave them just yet; they need me*. I looked back up at Jesus and said, "I have to go back, my girls are young and my husband will have no clue what to do!" He chuckled at that remark and nodded. He then laid His hand on my head one last time and I closed my eyes, soaking it all in while I could. When I opened my eyes again, I was right back in my hospital bed. My headache and chills returned, but this time, I knew what would heal me. Jesus told me what to ask for. *Lasix and potassium.* I called the nurse to get a doctor to put in an order for those medications. Surprisingly, they allowed it and once the medication was in, my body slowly started to stabilize. I even urinated for the first time in over three days about ten minutes after the first dose of Lasix was administered. A couple of doctors from the CDC asked me, "How did you know these meds would help you?" I told them what happened, to the best of my ability and surprisingly, the look on their faces said they believed me. I was so sick and the fact that these two pills were what I needed to recover...there was no other word for it but a miracle.

To this day, I still connect with these beings I met that day in the golden field. They show themselves in the sky to make it known that they are always with me. And Jesus has held my hand every step of the way in my journey back to health. Since my near-death experience, I have lost over 140 pounds and reversed all of my pre-existing health issues. I am now the healthiest I have ever been. I live for my family and my friends, but most importantly, for myself. I live for that girl who almost died that day but was saved - because my story is not finished.

Jacqueline Zralka - Reiki Master Teacher, Intuitive Channel of Healing

https://www.facebook.com/groups/healingwithangelsandintentionsgroup

https://www.facebook.com/Jacqueline.Middlecamp.Zralka

Root Into Your Power - The Masculine Will Rise With You

Janaki Mayhill

This is the whisper I hear through the water as my feet sink deep into the mud of the lake. The earth holds me. Something ancient moves through the stillness, a truth landing deep within my BEing.

During this time my husband is in the hospital fighting necrotizing fasciitis. Doctors are preparing to amputate his right big toe. Life feels fragile and uncertain, yet something sacred is beginning to unfold.

Around this time I am planning my annual women's retreat **Sounds of Soul**, a sacred space where women embrace their full selves. This year I feel drawn toward Bali, yet something inside me says not yet. The place meant to hold this gathering has not revealed itself.

So I call it in.
I write a declaration in my journal.

"I have the most aligned location for Sounds of Soul for the ultimate perspective of all within seventy-two hours."

When I finish writing, I pause.
Why did I write seventy-two hours?
Still, I release attachment and trust what moved through me.

Later that day I sit in the bathtub surrounded by candlelight with my journals, as I soak and write in gratitude. Then a message moves through me with unmistakable clarity. **The more I say yes to me and my sovereignty, the more I feel received.**

TRUTH moves through my entire body.
"This is what unlocks humanity."

A few days later I attend a friend's baby shower. During conversation I begin sharing about the retreat. My friend's beloved listens quietly and then says something unexpected. "Why don't you have it at my place in Guatemala?" He shows me photos of his Earthship at Lake Atitlán. The moment I see them my whole body lights up. The Mayans call it the belly button of the Earth.

Then I realize, it is still within the seventy-two hours.

Several women initially say yes to joining, yet one by one they withdraw. Confusion moves through me, yet I know this journey is meant to happen.

The next morning I lie in bed and speak directly to God. "If Sounds of Soul is meant to happen, I call in four hundred dollars for my plane ticket."

A few hours later someone messages asking if I need money and sends four hundred dollars—exactly the amount I spoke.. A few days later a soul brother offers a family constellation water reading. The message becomes clear.

Yes, I am meant to go to Guatemala.
The journey is not for everyone else.
It is for me.

Tears fill my eyes. "This scares the shit out of me," I say out loud.

Less than a week later I arrived in Antigua with nowhere to stay. Every hostel is full. Then I find one last minute. When I finally reach Lake Atitlán something in my body softens. Mountains rise around the water like quiet guardians and the air feels alive.

Even though I am moving through sciatic pain in my back, I continue walking the steep mountain paths. Something inside me knows I am meant to be here.

The first night I begin singing softly. "Now secure foundation, rooted and sovereign love." As I sing, fireworks burst across the sky over the lake. The moment I finish, the fireworks stop. I laugh quietly. Life is speaking back.

The next day a hummingbird flies into my friend's home. He gently releases it back into the sky. The following day I attend an Ecstatic Dance gathering where a Maya elder guides a fire ceremony. As seeds crackle in the flames, one suddenly pops from the fire and kisses my cheek.

The shaman points directly at me. "You stabilize your wealth," he says.

That same night one of my shoes disappear. When I finally release my attachment to it, the shoe appears again. As we walk up the mountain toward his home, it suddenly breaks. I laugh, realizing the mountain may be asking me to walk a new path.

The next morning we discover a small bird that has died inside the house, as if another cycle is quietly completing itself. Later my friend and I sit together writing in our journals, naming what we no longer tolerate and what we are calling into our lives. Right as we finish writing, a large black scorpion appears beside us.

We pause. Instead of fear, I feel reverence, as if the land itself is witnessing our declaration.

That night I pull a card that says **Breakthrough**. Later a strong gust of wind moves through the room and sends another card flying to the ground. The word on it is **Integration**.

The next morning we light a small fire and burn what we no longer carry. Looking back, it feels the elements themselves were guiding me.

When I return home the sciatic pain intensifies and I can barely stand. Yet this breakdown becomes the doorway to another revelation. I find myself locked out, as if everything has shifted so quickly I no longer know where I belong, even questioning whether my marriage still aligns with who I am becoming.

The next morning, on my birthday, I choose myself fully, ready to honor my truth even if it means giving my marriage a sacred pause.

Later that day I receive a spontaneous spinal flow session. As she works on me tears stream down my face while energy begins moving through my body.

Later I share everything with my husband. He wraps his arms around me. For the first time in months I feel held instead of being the one holding everyone else. In that moment everything comes full circle.

The retreat I thought I was creating for other women was never about them.
It was an initiation for me.
Choosing myself did not break my life.
It restored it.

When we choose ourselves, life reorganizes around our TRUTH. I finally understand the whisper I heard standing in the lake.

Root into your power.
Life rises with you.

That is the miracle.

Janaki Mayhill - Soul Architect
https://bhaktilight.com
https://linktree.com/bhaktilight

The Day My Daughter Called Me

Janet Charette

I was estranged from my daughter for almost nine years.

At some point, I accepted that family just wouldn't be a part of my life. I stopped hoping. I stopped letting myself feel the ache. I threw myself into service and healing work. I got good at guiding others. Deep down, I had buried the one desire I couldn't admit: that I still longed to belong.

During a Heart Freedom Weekend with Dr. Lise Janelle, she gently asked, "Why didn't you include family in your life purpose?"

I didn't even hesitate. I told her, "Because I don't believe it is possible. Why bother setting yourself up for disappointment?"

That moment was painful. But it was also freeing. I wasn't lying to myself anymore. For the first time in years, I allowed myself to feel what my heart truly wanted.

I said it out loud that I want to be connected.
I want to be in my daughter's life.

I want to be a grandmother who helps her family co-regulate.
It matters. I matter. And I deserve love.

That moment of truth changed everything.

My daughter reached out almost immediately. Perhaps some invisible switch had flipped. It was unexpected and "automagical." We didn't try to fix everything. We just began playing it by feel.

It started with short, simple conversations followed by photos, laughter, even plans to see each other again.

And here I am, after nearly a decade of silence, celebrating Christmas with my daughter and my grandsons. We're going on a road trip together. And Grandma Cookie (that's me) is the one who helps everyone co-regulate in the car.

I've become a resource in her life. She calls when things get overwhelming. I don't try to control anything. I just hold space instead of holding back. We move in rhythm again.

That's the miracle. The miracle isn't that she changed.

It's that I did.

I learned how to stay in my body through the grief. I thawed the part of me that believed it wasn't safe to want love, I stopped rejecting the possibility. I let the Creator show me what was ready to return. I softened enough to let it in.

There were still moments of fear and trembling. There were times I could feel my trauma response wanting to shut me down, wanting to freeze. But this time, I stayed.

I used the Heart Freedom tools I had been learning. I called on "Compassionkey" and somatic tracking and I gave my younger self compassion instead of criticism. And I didn't disappear. I didn't need to be right or to prove anything. I let love be more important than the story I used to tell.

We're not pretending everything is fine. We're building something real. We're learning from each other again. That's the deeper miracle:the slow kind, the lived kind.

If you've been estranged from your child or your grandchildren, please know: Your story isn't over.

You don't have to pretend you don't care. You don't have to shut down hope just to protect yourself. You get to tell the truth about what you want, even if it hurts. You get to soften.

Miracles aren't always loud.

Sometimes they whisper.
Sometimes they arrive as a message out of the blue.
And sometimes they come the moment you stop performing and start receiving.

This year, the miracle wasn't that I got my daughter back...It was that I stayed in my body long enough to receive her when she returned.

I let myself be loved.
I let myself matter.

And this year, I get to hear "Grandma!" from the backseat of a car filled with laughter, snow falling on the windows and love in the in-between spaces.

I used to think miracles were for other people.

Now I know... They're for those of us who stay.

Janet Charette - Freedom Whisperer
http://bit.ly/3YZePH7
thebookonovercomingoverwhelm.com

Miracles & True Fairytale Love

Jennifer Rogers Markwell

I used to believe that love had to be dramatic to be real... Disney Princess, movie-worthy, electric, chaotic... But as it turns out, real love is even better. Stronger. Rooted in purpose. And sometimes, it begins on a night you never planned, at a dinner you didn't want to attend.

I met my husband on a blind date that neither of us wanted to go on.

He was divorced, protective of his heart, and even more protective of his daughter. I was fresh out of one of the most heartbreaking seasons of my life, grieving the loss of my beloved grandfather, my Poppy, and caring for my Gram, who had lost her partner of 65 years. Romance was the furthest thing from either of our minds.

We were both tired. Not the kind of tired that sleep fixes, but the kind that sits behind your eyes and deep in your chest — the kind that comes from carrying too much for too long. He had been navigating single fatherhood with quiet determination, doing school drop-offs, packing lunches, all while trying to heal from a marriage that hadn't survived. I, in turn, had walked away from a long, successful career in television to be present for my family and to start over in an entirely new field. We were both building new lives, piece by piece.

So when a mutual friend insisted and wouldn't take no for an answer, we reluctantly agreed. (Mostly to get him off our backs). I remember walking into the wine bar and spotting him at a table. He stood up as I approached, a little nervous, a little unsure, but with kind eyes and a gentle smile that put me at ease. What started out as polite conversation turned into something deeper. We just talked about life; it was electric. Such an intense spark that was wildly noticeable.

He spoke about his daughter like she was his whole world, and I felt something in me soften. Not because he was perfect, but because he was real. He was grounded. Present. There was no ego, no show, just an honest man doing the best he could. And he was funny. (That was always at the top of my list; *must make me laugh*). We both laughed so hard that night.

And maybe that's what caught me off guard. I wasn't expecting a miracle that night. But sometimes, miracles show up when you least expect them. I had met the man who would change my life.

We were 'all in' almost immediately and engaged two months later.

Yes, it was fast. We didn't tell anyone other than my Gram and his dad. For us, it just made sense. When you have learned how precious time is, you don't waste it. And four months after that first date, we were married. It was a whirlwind, yes. It was right. It went deeper than butterflies. We just knew.

And then, because life loves a little magic, he proposed again. This time in Scotland. He had planned the trip. He dropped to one knee and asked me to choose him again. "I want forever with you. Not just once—but over and over." I said yes. Through tears. Through laughter. Through complete awe.

That moment didn't replace our original proposal at the dining room table — it deepened it. It became our vow: to keep falling in love, to keep choosing each other, no matter the season. And we have kept that vow—literally.

In the eleven years since we married, we renewed our vows over 30 times. In big cities, on quiet beaches, while completing international bucket lists, over surprise weekends and even on ordinary days in our backyard. It was his idea. He said, "I always want our love to be front and center."

Each vow renewal is a pause in our chaotic lives... a celebration of us. Sometimes we wear a white dress and a tux. Sometimes we are in our best Star Wars attire. It doesn't matter what we wear. What matters is that we show up, again and again and say: "I still do." He met Gram early on, and she adored him. And his daughter? She became the brightest surprise of all. Our bond developed instantly—through runway walks, tea parties and a shared love of her dad. She didn't just become a part of my life. She became a part of my heart.We didn't build our family in the traditional way. We built it our way.

I used to think that miracles were rare; only reserved for the very lucky. Now, I know better.

They show up in whirlwind romances that feel like coming home or in second chances that arrive when you're not looking; in grand gestures on foreign soil; in handwritten vows whispered again and again.

And every time we say "I do" whether for the 31st time or the 301st time — it is a reminder that:

Miracles are normal.

Jennifer Rogers Markwell - Emmy® Nominated Wealth Advisor & President at Platinum Wealth Management

www.PlatinumWealth.net

https://www.linkedin.com/in/jennifer-rogers-markwell-cpfa%C2%AE-64aa6b10/

I Am Going To The Rainforest

Jenny Treurnich

I was sitting on a hard bench in a quiet corner of Cape Town International Airport, my suitcase at my feet, my phone clutched in my hand, oscillating between hope and despair.

Around me, the airport hummed with movement, yet time felt suspended. I had been sitting there for hours, trying to buy the only airline ticket on the one flight that could get me to Costa Rica in time. And my bank kept blocking the transaction.

I kept repeating the same sentence silently, like a thread holding me together, *"I am going to the rainforest"*.

I had booked a retreat in the Costa Rican rainforest months earlier. I was excited with every fibre of my being. I would meet coaches I had only known through screens: women I longed to hug and share space with. Stillness, going within, community. And excited because the rainforest itself had lived in me since childhood.

I had checked visa requirements, bought my ticket, packed provisions. Everything seemed aligned – until I tried to check in and was told I could not board. I needed a transit visa. The moment landed like a physical blow. I stepped out of the line, standing there with my luggage, stunned, devastated and close to tears.

The next 8 hours were a blur of airport counters, phone calls, online searches back at home, and conflicting information. Could I reach Costa Rica and not miss more than one night of the retreat, without *any* transit visas? The odds were impossibly slim. My daughter and two of the coaches held unwavering faith that I would get there.

I kept repeating the mantra – sometimes with conviction, sometimes with desperation: *"I am going to the rainforest"*.

The following morning, a travel agent confirmed that it was possible to transit air-side: one stop – not two. There was exactly one viable flight left. One seat. To take it, I first had to get from Cape Town to Johannesburg. I had now returned to the airport, running on faith and adrenaline and had tried repeatedly to buy the flight. The situation was painfully delicate. There were two possible local flights to Johannesburg: only the first one guaranteed enough time. Seats were disappearing.

Then a woman sat down beside me. Allison.

She didn't need to be there. She could have gone through security, found a comfortable chair, had a coffee... Instead, she stayed on that hard bench next to me. She listened. And then she asked, "Could your bank be blocking the payment thinking it's fraud?" She was right. I called the fraud department repeatedly. Each time they assured me that it had been resolved. Each time the payment failed. The first local flight departed. My stress escalated, but Allison stayed – calm and present.

She insisted I buy the local ticket. It vanished from my phone. Close to tears, I bought the local ticket at the counter and checked in just before it closed. I was now operating on trust, universal law, and sheer hope. We went through security together. At the gate, boarding had begun. I had 10 minutes.

Then Allison offered to pay for my international ticket – R25,000 – I could pay her back once I reached Johannesburg.

A stranger. I have no words for the gratitude that filled me.

We tried to book the flight. It also disappeared. A rush of adrenaline. It reappeared. She almost clicked on a flight with 2 stops. Officials were calling me. Passengers were already waiting on a bus.

And then... it went through. I scribbled her details down, hugged her quickly and ran for the gate.

At the international desk in Johannesburg, passport in hand, heart pounding, I was checked through to Costa Rica.

I stood there, stunned. Against logic. Against probability... I was going to the rainforest.

I ran through security and paid Allison back via my phone as my flight boarded. The rest unfolded smoothly: Paris air-side, no visa needed. Somewhere over the Atlantic, my body finally exhaled completely. A smile spread across my face as something deep inside of me settled.

A stranger had appeared in exactly the right place, at exactly the right time.

I was used to being the one helping other women navigate crossroads in life; helping them manifest what their hearts were yearning for; helping them remember who they truly are at a soul level.

This time, I had to let go. Surrender. Trust. Allow someone else to steady me – whilst still holding belief.

I had to dance with both my human and my divine, constantly moving between the two.

This dream was too real, too raw, and had lived inside me for too long for me to hold certainty the entire time. But others held it for me: my daughter, the two soul-sister coaches, and Allison.

When we create together, we are unstoppable.

Miracles are not rare disruptions of reality. They are what happens when we truly follow our dreams: when we can hold the presence of possibility. And sometimes, when we can't, when we can stay present long enough for help to find us.

Jenny Treurnich - Mindset and Embodiment Coach
https://www.jennytreurnich.com
https://www.youtube.com/@JennyTreurnich

Grief To Groove - How I started The 'Groovement'

Jill Boychuk

In 2010 my mom, Connie or Constance, was diagnosed with inoperable Lung Cancer and passed away the following year in 2011, at the age of 70. My mom was a beautiful lady both inside and out and one who loved to sew; we sewed together when I was a young girl. We would spend hours together in that little sewing room in the basement of our house in Brandon, MB. She always loved to do crafts and to paint and she turned her passion into an art.

We talked about that, and other things about life on that beautiful, sunny, breezy day at our family cottage at Clear Lake, MB. What is life? What is it about? What are some of the things she regretted? What are some of the things I want to live by?

I mentioned that I wanted to combine my passions and I felt that there was something more than being a Dental Hygienist all my life. I was a runner and I ran many races in marathons around the world. What's next, I thought to myself - I was 41 years old at this point; what could contribute to my life and to others, and how could I honor my mom and create a legacy to leave behind? I went for a run in my favorite place at the lake down around Deep Bay to meditate on these questions.

Thinking back on my childhood and on all the things I loved to do... I loved sports, crafts, adventure, playing outside with nature, being spontaneous and sewing with my mom... but most of all, being creative. What if I could combine art on fabric and sewing... would that be possible? It was a faraway dream - or was it?

My mom told me three things that I now live by every day... she quietly whispers them in my ear when I need to hear them:

-Don't regret anything

-Don't hold anger in you

-Just do it - don't overthink it, just figure it out.

From that day forward I decided to figure it out! I trusted the Universe and where I was about to head, and I started to navigate my ship in the direction I wanted it to go in my life. I started off using local seamstresses working from their homes. Slowly I started designing prints by drawing or using pictures to form the feel I wanted. Somehow, miraculously, I got everything done in a week.

I showed up at my first sale at the Nordic Centre in Canmore, AB on Mother's Day weekend at the Rocky Mountain Women's Run for Women's Health. I stood on top of that mountain and looked out at the beautiful nature; the sun was shining brightly and I cried happy tears. I had done it. I had broken through my fears and produced something to share with others at an event. I got a taste of what was possible and on my drive home I decided that my life was going to be a journey of discovery and learning.

Another miracle was unfolding. I met the magic for our creations, Candie.

She answered the door, all 4 feet 10 of her with her cute glasses perched on her nose. I said, "I want to do an athletic line, put designs on fabric, produce better items for others, and make a difference doing it. I need your help. Are you open to seeing what we can do together?" Candie replied, saying, "Why not? Let's see where this goes", and that was the beginning of a new reality. Candie started to work on samples. We would draw or visualize items starting very slowly, one pattern at a time.

Earthgroove Activewear was born. Ambassadors started to show up who loved the product and it spread by word of mouth. Miracle after miracle was unfolding that aligned with our energy.

The crazy thing is how in sync Lisa, my graphic designer and Candie and I are, as most days we would wake up with the same thoughts of what to do next and how we could make it better. It's a match made in heaven.

We are proud to say we give back to mental health and other initiatives through the brand; we support the community by attending events, collaborating with many companies and we sell online.

Brooklyn, my daughter, designs and is the Creative Director of the company and my son Blake, is taking on the website changes and marketing. It is a family affair and a legacy that is generational. We are helping the local economy and community and helping others to heal through the brand.

My mom is my guiding light every day and shows me the way. I have a tattoo of the sun on my left shoulder and as I look up into the sky when I see the sun, I know I am looked after. Before she passed, my mom said it would be her sign that she is around. Thanks Mom, we are doing great things together... we are changing the world and making it better, one step at a time. Thank you for believing in me.

Jill Boychuk - Owner/Designer of Earthgroove Activewear

https://www.instagram.com/earthgrooveactivewear

https://earth-groove.com

How I Helped Iyanla Attract Oprah

Julia Stege

I will never forget the day in 2010 when I checked my voicemail and heard, "Hi! It's Iyanla. I got your Magical Toolkit and I want my fifteen minutes!"

I actually froze.

Just recently I had been trying to find out what had happened to Iyanla Vanzant. I loved her on *The Oprah Show*, known as 'The Guru from the Hood', and then she disappeared. No one I asked knew how to reach her.

And now she was calling *me*. Out of the blue!

Just a couple of weeks earlier, I had attended a Law of Attraction retreat where I got a crystal clear vision: *'I want to uplift and empower millions of people to transform the world.'*

The problem was that my upcoming class had only 6 registrations.

Six.

I remember thinking, *how exactly does this scale to millions?* But when I looked at my coach, his eyes told me, "It is done!"

At the same time, I was interviewing entrepreneurs for a book on manifesting breakthroughs and I kept feeling nudged to interview Iyanla. But no one knew where she was or how to reach her. I let it go all the while still holding the intention.

Two weeks later, there she was, scheduling a session. But I didn't know it was her. On my intake form she was listed under her maiden name, and she had said she was an EFT life coach, not a bestselling author!

When we finally spoke, we talked for over an hour before I started reviewing her website and I noticed that she was selling Iyanla Vanzant books. "Oh, you're selling Iyanla Vanzant books," I said, completely clueless and in denial.

"Yes," she said calmly.

"Well," I replied, "I think *'In the Meantime'* is one of the best relationship books ever written."

"Thank you."

Pause.

"Wait... is that *you?*" I asked.

"Yes," she said gently. "I used my married name; you wouldn't have known."

I told her, "If I *had* known it was you, I would have been a lot less informal."

She laughed. "Oh, Julia, don't worry. I learned not to walk on water—it's bad for my Jimmy Choos."

Then she told me the truth about where she had been.

After leaving *The Oprah Show* for another network that didn't honor her vision, she lost that contract and a book deal. Her daughter became ill with cancer and Iyanla spent everything trying to save her. Her daughter passed away and shortly afterwards, her husband—the love of her life—left her via email. She lost her home. She came frighteningly close to ending her own life.

When we met, she was rebuilding from ashes, writing a book called *Peace from Broken Pieces* and trying to realign with the deeper reason she was here: to help people heal, find peace and to transform their lives.

We began working on her Attraction Plan, clarifying what mattered most and aligning everything with her true vision. Eventually, we worked on the website for her nonprofit, Inner Visions Worldwide. At that time, Iyanla had not spoken with Oprah in nearly a decade.

Then, one day in February 2011, Iyanla called me.

Oprah had invited her to her final show to be interviewed about Peace from Broken Pieces.

We had two weeks to make the website 'Oprah-ready.'

I was ecstatic. "That's exactly what you wanted!"

She paused. "Well," she said, "my guides said that this was the best way to get my vision to the world." Yes, she was going to speak her transformational vision to millions of people - and I had helped.

When the show came on, I was actually on the phone with Iyanla talking about what had happened behind the scenes. What was clear to me on that day was that both of our Attraction Plans had come true.

After those interviews, Oprah gave Iyanla her own show which played a major role in stabilizing the OWN network. It was not I who transformed the lives of those millions but I had supported Iyanla at a key moment using the Attraction Plan and the container of a new website.

This miracle came because I had set an intention and I had let it go. That intention matched with Iyanla's intention to get her vision out to the world.

Here is what I know for sure: miracles don't come from forcing outcomes. They come from alignment, from remembering your vision and from making choices that honor who you truly are.

The Attraction Plan I used with Iyanla is the same one I have shared with thousands of people who felt called to something bigger than their current circumstances. When you align with the future that's already waiting for you, life has a remarkable way of meeting you there.

And that?

That's when miracles become normal.

Julia Stege - Magical Marketer
https://magical-marketing-company.mykajabi.com/getstap
https://www.facebook.com/julia.stege

Touched By Divine Hands

Julianna Rose

Miracles often arrive like invisible hands moving through our realities, reminding us of our sacred bond with the Creator. My life is a testament to these mystical cosmic forces guided by the greater unknown. These events, known as miracles, have been normal for me. But three stood out as profound experiences steeped in deep, unconditional love. Through their life-altering intervention, I renewed my faith in the Creator, reconnected to my soul's path, and awakened to the divine orchestration guiding my sacred mission. Each miracle brought me closer to my purpose, not just as an individual, but as part of a greater union, one that would later manifest through love, abundance, and partnership with my beloved husband.

The first miracle came on a midsummer's day. The sun beamed its promise of warmth to all life from high in the sky. I was a young girl, free-spirited and curious. I remember sitting in the back seat of my parents' old car, on my older brother's lap, with no seat belt. My hands reached for the shiny chrome handle, and I started to turn. Before I knew it, the door flew open, and I tumbled onto the pavement as the car went around the bend.

Time stopped, and my life flashed before me. Screams rang out of my mouth simultaneously as tires screeched. I was dangerously close to death by giant metallic bumpers. Yet, amidst the chaos, something unexplainable happened—a protective bubble surrounded me seconds before the cars swerved, missing my fragile form by mere inches.

I survived with only minor bumps and bruises, but the experience left a permanent, impressionable mark on my soul. In retrospect, it wasn't just a stroke of luck, but a divine shield of love and a testament to the unseen guardians always with us. I was too young to articulate it, but my soul recognized the sacred hand intervening and ensuring I remained safe in my earthly journeys.

Years later, as a teenager, the Creator made its presence known. It was a warm night filled with reckless adventure. My friends and I piled into another old car, laughing and singing as we sped along the highway. Then, in an instant, our carefree night turned into a game of survival.

The driver lost control of the wheel, the car swerved violently, and the next thing I knew, we were trapped under heaps of crushed metal. Gas was spilling out of the tank, sending waves of fear through us. We managed to kick the glass out of a window, escaping with minor bumps and bruises. We were shaken but unharmed.

Again, amid the chaos, I felt the same mysterious energies as before creating a protective cocoon around us. Instantly, I was made aware that even when the physical world threatens to crumble, the divine is always there to hold us, like a cosmic cushion. This was another supernatural occurrence connected to something far greater than you or me, keeping life preserved and in harmony.

The final intervention came during our "global pause." I was battling COVID, my body weakened by pneumonia, my spirit dimmed by uncertainty. Each breath was a struggle, and I was hanging on by a thin thread, fighting for a life I wasn't ready to leave.

I turned to the Creator and the guardians I sensed around me. I prayed and surrendered, opening myself to the unknown mysteries of healing and renewal. I gave a simple, powerful plea: "I am ready to be healed and continue my soul's work. Please guide me back to the light of my life."

What followed was nothing short of miraculous. I felt an infusion of light warming my chest and radiating outward, as though the invisible hands were mending me back together again. My recovery accelerated in ways that I couldn't explain. Cell by cell, my body healed and repaired itself. Even though it took several months, my mind awakened to a deeper truth of unbreakable trust in the Creator. I was being prepared for the next phase of my divine mission, one that would no longer be walked alone but *hand-in-hand* with my beloved husband. The Creator was aligning us in our sacred partnership, where we would become a vessel of higher service to help others create their abundant life.

Every miracle thus far has been a guidepost, an initiation marker into greater trust and alignment with the divine plan unfolding before me. Each touch has led me closer to my soul's highest path—a path I now walk with the love of my life. Together, we are co-creating our life of abundance, weaving miracles into every aspect of our shared journey, and uplifting the world through our beautiful union. As our unified vision harmonizes with joyful purpose, our soul connection deepens, igniting and strengthening the Creator's energy within us and guiding us toward a destiny of building limitless abundance through our wealth education business. A destiny I hadn't recognized before, yet now I realize it was written and designed long before we ever met.

Months have passed since my beloved and I merged with our missions. Now comes the real work and the day-to-day tasks for us to serve the higher calling and to share the wisdom of wealth and abundance with those who are ready to receive it. These are the ordinary, mundane tasks that create lasting prosperity for our communities. The step-by-step process and plan of action we design to communicate our message and philosophy. They are the building blocks of our miracles and require laser-like focus and commitment, whether we are comfortable with it or not. For us, it's an endless wave of expansion and contraction, stretching and withdrawing of our joined consciousness to reach our goals. It begins as soon as we rise from our beds and start the daily dream of abundance living in the scenes of our minds and the sensations in our bodies.

We journal our thoughts, imagining all the lives we positively impact through our service work, and feeling the infinite possibilities grow in our imaginations. We read books that increase our financial literacy. We study the wellness habits of the wealthy and apply their techniques to protect and preserve our income. We attend self-improvement events to learn the skills others have mastered. We gather with teammates and share our wins.

Above all, we connect to gratitude in our hearts for the abundance the Creator has already provided for us and the wealth on its way. And gratitude for helping others fulfill their dreams and goals. Those are the moments we feel truly blessed to experience. As a result, our abundance mission is strengthened, our financial education business is established, and our wealth legacy is rooted.

On this journey to abundance, our mission is to educate people in the money game and share proven steps to prosperity. We discuss the different vehicles they can use to support their family's financial goals, showing them ways to avoid harmful debt, save consistently, and invest intentionally. We also teach them the importance of self-improvement through positive thinking, encouragement, and assured belief in the Creator's plan.

For us, it's not just about acquiring money for its use as a physical tool in exchange for goods and services. It's also about money as an energetic currency, for good, on a path of soul ascension. By providing this money education platform, we can fill the hearts of many with high-frequency wealth keys that unlock the financial freedom the soul deeply craves and provide them with an inner peace that illuminates their path of miracles.

Even in the brilliance of this new chapter of miracles in our storybook of life, challenges arise. Far too often, we meet beautiful souls who have been deeply traumatized by scarcity, and they hesitate and resist their path of abundance. Conditioned by fear and limitation, money feels heavy, like a burden, not a blessing. We know these blocks aren't permanent, but initiation markers of greater financial freedom. So, we go gently, meeting people where they are with compassion and empathy, unraveling the wounds of money, clearing outdated financial beliefs, and liberating the flow of wealth in their thinking.

How often can one say that they get to help families rewrite their money stories and ignite the miracle energy of true abundance within their hearts?

As trailblazers, my beloved and I are scripting a new era of purpose-driven prosperity. This is the awakening that our wealth-building team is teaching others. We are transforming the financial world bit by bit. And it feels as if we've done this before, perhaps in another realm or lifetime where we were also sent as creator architects of abundance, guiding others to rise into their highest potential of prosperity, refining their frequency bandwidth as we go. Unified in purpose and leadership, we see our clients succeed and our dreams of financial freedom take form. It is nothing short of miraculous— a breathtaking unfolding of truth, love, and higher purpose.

In my opinion, our souls were always meant to experience the infinite flow of prosperity, for prosperity is part of our soul's inheritance. I believe that the divine right of humanity is to work with money as a sacred medium of exchange for financial freedom, legacy building, and generational wealth. This is the powerful message that we are called to share and teach: that the struggle is never just external, it is internal. Every challenge is an opportunity to rise to our greatness. And when you do, you rise into miracles because they are your birthright. Miracles are not the exception; they are normal. And as our trust in the unseen grows, greater miracles appear.

I invite you to trust in the unseen, believe in the mystical, and know that you are always held in the graceful embrace of the Creator. Whether you walk this path alone or alongside a divine partner, miracles will find you. Simply allow yourself to receive the touch from divine hands.

Infinite love and abundance.

Julianna Rose - Spiritual Wealth Architect
www.jrosehealing.com
www.facebook.com/jrosehealing

Becoming The Miracle

Kat Bartlett

People often imagine miracles arriving in bright flashes of light or heavenly choirs, something unmistakably divine that interrupts life in an obvious way. Mine arrived much differently, holding two butcher knives and forcing a moment that would change everything I thought I understood about survival, faith and the quiet strength that grows inside a person, long before she realizes it.

The morning it happened, the world seemed to pause in that strange way where the air itself feels aware that something is about to unfold. At the time I did not yet understand the significance of the moment but I was standing on the edge between the life I had been surviving and the life that was about to begin.

For years I had prayed for a miracle. I imagined some kind of intervention that would calm the chaos around me and make everything safe again. What I came to understand later is that miracles rarely arrive in the way people expect. Sometimes they appear as a turning point, the moment when everything becomes clear enough that you can finally see the truth of the life you have been living.

That morning, just days before I was supposed to remarry, my ex-husband found out and was on his way to kill my children and me. Police stopped him before he reached us and when they did, he was holding two butcher knives. He was shot before he could reach us. There was no doubt what would have happened if he had arrived first.

Many people would call that luck, but the longer I have lived with that moment, the more I understand it differently. I had prayed for protection for years without knowing what that protection would look like. Looking back now, I believe that morning was not a chance. It was the moment my life was redirected before something irreversible could happen.

I did not simply get out that day. I got up.

Getting up did not look heroic in the beginning. It looked like small choices made quietly when no one else was watching. It looked like learning to trust my instincts again after years of questioning myself and choosing peace over chaos, even when chaos had been the familiar thing for so long.

At first I did not feel strong. I felt exhausted and I was uncertain of who I even was outside of the life I had been trying so hard to hold together. Yet somewhere beneath the exhaustion something else was beginning to grow, a quiet determination that my story would not end the way it almost had.

Before that morning, my life had existed in a constant state of 'almost' safe. Living that way teaches you to read moods carefully and to anticipate storms before they arrive. Over time you begin adjusting yourself in quiet ways to avoid conflict until one day, you look in the mirror and you realize that the woman looking back at you has been shrinking for years.

There were evenings when I sat in the driveway after work with my hands resting on the steering wheel, gathering the courage to walk into my own home. During those years I was living with domestic violence that I never spoke about and worked carefully to hide from the outside world, even from my own children. There were mornings when I woke before sunrise simply to experience a few minutes of calm before the tension of the house returned with everyone else. I prayed for signs and answers, hoping for direction that would not require losing everything I had built.

What I understand now is that the signs had always been there. My body recognized the danger long before my mind allowed itself to acknowledge it, and my intuition had been speaking quietly for years. Survivors recognize this pattern immediately because leaving rarely happens when someone tells you to leave. It happens when something inside you finally refuses to stay.

In the years that followed I rebuilt my life one truth at a time. Healing did not happen overnight. It required counseling, reflection, community and time. And I made the decision to seek the help I needed so that I could understand what I had lived through and move forward with clarity.

Over time I learned to trust my own voice again. Survival slowly became something more than simply getting through each day. It became about living with truth, self-respect and the understanding that my life still belonged to me.

That journey eventually led me to create Kat's Kastle Foundation, a place where survivors of domestic violence can find dignity, support and community, as they rebuild their lives. It also led to the creation of I Got Out, a storytelling movement where survivors reclaim their voices and share the truth of what they have lived through.

For a long time I believed the miracle was simply the moment when the police stopped him before he reached us. That moment saved my life. The deeper miracle unfolded afterward in the quiet rebuilding that followed... in the courage to begin again... and in the realization that survival can grow into something far greater than the moment that first saved you.

Looking back now I understand something I could not see then:

The miracle was never only that I survived...The miracle was realizing that my life still belonged to me, and that the moment that once felt like an ending had quietly become the beginning of everything that followed.

Kat Bartlett - Creator of 'I Got Out' - The Movement
https://katskastlefoundation.com
https://www.amazon.com/dp/B0F8R87MRH

You Are A Miracle

Katie Carey

I have come to understand that miracles don't always arrive with rainbows and unicorns. Sometimes, they are disguised as loss, struggle, or a quiet whisper.

This is my journey through those moments and the truth that I have come to live by.

Miracles are normal.

Despite my struggles living with disabilities and chronic pain, there is one thing I choose daily...to acknowledge the miracles in my life.

My being here is a miracle.

I was born a rainbow baby, after the stillbirth of my brother. I have always believed that just being here is miraculous.

Even in a violence-filled childhood, I was seen as a daydreamer; singing, reading, escaping into music and stories. I believed that anything was possible. My dad encouraged my creativity, but he was also my biggest fear.

Raised Catholic, I prayed often and believed in angels from a young age. After my Nan passed, I asked God to let me see her and she came to me in dreams. That connection with spirit felt like a miracle.

From the age of 9 to 18, I lived two lives: fear at home; and a dream life on stage; acting, singing, dancing and gymnastics. I won awards and was presented with a silver medal by Olympic medalist David Moorcroft, who even coached me in pole vaulting.

Things changed when I married a soldier. He was rarely home and when he was, he tried to control everything. But my three children were miracles. I showed up for them daily.

Still, I was constantly juggling debts and my creativity went unused for years. Eventually, I found some stability. I worked multiple unfulfilling jobs but quietly began building online businesses, singing again and using my gifts where I could.

After divorcing, I believed I had found my soulmate. It felt magical at first until I realised he was an alcoholic. Losing my father to addiction had left me hyper-vigilant and this felt all too familiar. Life felt heavy until I walked into a meditation class at work.

Soon after, I discovered Dr. Joe Vitale, whose work reminded me that miracles were real and that I was one of them. I began studying holistic therapies while earning a degree. I became a mindfulness coach, trained in the Law of Attraction, Ho'oponopono, Belief Clearing and more. I even founded an alternative holistic mental health charity.

But as my alignment deepened, my body began to hurt. It is clear now with hindsight that the job and the marriage no longer fitted the reality I was creating.

I was afraid to let go but the Universe intervened, disabling me and forcing me to stop. In that stillness, I saw clearly. Both marriages had made me deeply unwell. Some might call it failure, divorce, illness, early retirement.

But it was the beginning of returning to myself.

What looked like painful endings were really redirections. When I shifted my thinking, life no longer felt like a battle. Every moment became a miracle.

I reconnected with the version of myself who had always known that miracles are normal. I now let my creative gifts flow through conversations, poetry, books and songs. They move people, just as they move me.

Since 2020, miracles have shown up for me again and again. Sometimes in beauty; sometimes in hardships...but always, miracles.

Ten people can look at the same thing and see something different. I choose to notice awe in the small things...to live in the frequency of miracles. Signs and synchronicities leap out at me, often several times a day. And when they do, I feel them. I acknowledge them with love. This awareness has opened doors that others have walked past. Why? Because they believe they're not ready, not good enough, or that it is not meant for them. These are limiting beliefs, brakes on the soul's next intuitive nudge.

But what if you could flip the switch and remember...

You are ready.
You are enough.
You are a co-creator with God, Source, the Universe.
And everything is possible.

What if you accepted all of yourself?
What if you remembered that the very fact you are alive right now is a miracle?
Your heartbeat supports this planet without needing to prove or to chase anything.
What if you dropped the masks you've been wearing, to fit in?
What if being yourself was enough? Enough for your people to feel your energy. Enough to stop pretending in places that don't serve you.

You are a gift.
You are a miracle.

You have wisdom to share. You are the ripple that touches everyone around you, online or in person. Your words matter. Your heart matters. Loving yourself matters.

As the theme song of my podcast says, "You've Gotta Love Yourself."

So here is my challenge to you:

Start your next day knowing that miracles are normal. Notice each one. Feel them. Celebrate them. You are loved. You are blessed. You are a miracle and miracles are normal.

Katie Carey - Founder of Soulful Valley Publishing House & Podcast Featured in the Zero Limits Movie.
https://pensight.com/x/soulfulvalley
https://apple.co/3BkJdkn

LIFE IS MAGIC

Kelz Morris-Dale

When we think of miracles, we picture the extraordinary — beating cancer or winning the lottery. But what about the tiny, everyday moments that quietly change everything? Those fleeting moments that whisper: *You are loved, you are needed, you are seen.*

For me, miracles were once hard to believe in. Over the last few years, I have faced traumatic heartbreak and challenges, many rooted in my relationships. These experiences, often triggered by external parties, pushed me to the edge. At my lowest, I distinctly remember when the Barbie movie came out in 2023, I was in a dark place, feeling unnecessary and convinced that my kids didn't need or want me anymore.

Yes, it was that bad.

But life, as it often does, had other plans.

That movie came out over a year and a half ago, and since then, I have been on a journey of healing, growth, and rediscovery. The challenges didn't disappear, but I began to find joy in the smallest of moments—moments that felt magical, as though the Universe was sending me little love notes to keep me going.

One such moment happened recently. My daughter said, "Love you, Mum," without me saying it first. It had been a while since those words came unprompted, and I cannot describe the joy I felt. On the outside, I stayed cool, but inside, I was glowing. It felt like the best day of my life.

Then, as if the Universe wanted to give me another gift, my other daughter cuddled up to me at the movie theatre. She grabbed my hand, linked her fingers through mine, and rested her head on my shoulder. That moment felt magical. For the first time in a long time, I felt like a true mum again. I know I'm their mum, but in that moment, I truly felt needed and wanted—beyond just being someone who drives them to places or makes them endless snacks. I felt like they genuinely wanted me around. And I know people might say, "they're teenagers, it's normal," but I know there's been more to it than that. These small shifts feel monumental after everything we've been through. I'll continue to believe in the miraculous change in our relationship—because no one can stop a mum who loves her kids with unwavering strength!

To someone else, these moments may seem like small gestures, but to me, they are proof that miracles don't have to be grand. They can be as simple as a touch, a word, or a fleeting connection.

And while these moments with my daughters are incredibly special, they are just one part of the journey. There have been other miracles too, each one shaping me into the person I am today.

Overcoming divorce stands out as one of the most transformative. Divorce stripped me of who I thought I was, forcing me to rediscover who I truly am. While the process was painful, it awakened me to the magic of being whole on my own.

The death of my dad, another pivotal moment, broke me in ways I didn't think possible. Yet, in the midst of my grief, I began to notice hummingbirds everywhere — symbols of his presence, reminding me to breathe, to notice the beauty around me and to keep going.

Standing up to my mum after years of narcissistic abuse was yet another miracle. For years, I silenced my voice to keep the peace, but becoming a mother gave me the strength to set boundaries and protect my children. That act of courage was a miracle in itself — proof that healing and growth are possible, even in the most difficult relationships.

Through all of this, I have come to see myself in a new light. I am no longer defined by what others think of me. I am not just a mother, a daughter, or a wife. I am *me*... a magical, resilient being, capable of facing life's challenges and finding joy in its miracles.

This realization has brought me hope and peace in ways I never thought possible. My life isn't perfect, but it is full of magic. The kind of magic that reminds me that I am never alone, even in the darkest moments.

I share these experiences because I don't want anyone else to feel like they must face the darkness alone. Life can feel impossibly hard, but in the cracks of that pain, magic finds a way to enter. Miracles don't have to be grand gestures; they are found in the whispered words of a child, the warmth of a touch, and the quiet realization that you are still needed, still loved and still seen. That is why I'm here—to remind you that even in your lowest moments, there is beauty waiting to be discovered, and the magic of life will always find you.

What tiny miracles are waiting for you today?

Kelz Morris-Dale – Reiki Master & Soulful Marketing Mentor

https://linktr.ee/kelzthekiwi

https://www.facebook.com/kelz.morris.dale

Appreciating The Small Miracles = Magic Every Day

Krista Young

Sitting with friends at a local lakefront pub-style restaurant on a Saturday evening, the dinner conversation turned to the weather forecast.

Well into a particularly heavy winter, which had arrived earlier than usual with already record-breaking amounts of snowfall, it was interesting to hear the different perspectives about the pending storm.

Three friends, who all work for the school board, were excited and hopeful that Monday would be declared a "snow day" and schools would be closed. Another, who already had that day off, was indifferent about it.

Hearing one of them refer to what was coming as "snowmageddon" had me feeling both wistful and a bit wary for a few reasons:

1. With several exciting projects on the go, I had not truly had a free day just for myself in a while; a full day off would be wonderful!

2. My Sunday plans included clearing out all contents of my laundry room and front entrance to allow for final home renovations to be completed; loading personal belongings into my car, driving to a friend's house where I would be living for the next two weeks to take care of her cat while she was on vacation; and bringing said belongings into her house. Driving, loading and unloading in a blizzard would be unpleasant at best.

3. I had scheduled in-person time at a client's home, which was a 40 minute drive through rural country roads, on Monday; it's important to me to honour my commitments; at the same time, blizzard conditions would be a valid reason to re-schedule.

As I listened to my friends talk about how they would spend a "snow day" off work, I noticed my thoughts and emotions wobble back and forth between wistfully wanting and fiercely not wanting Monday to be a "snow day". Before the conversation moved on to other topics, I had decided that while I would absolutely love an entire day off to myself, I had to acknowledge that I have absolutely no control over the weather and as such, I would just go with the flow and see what happens.

And... the blizzard happened alright. It began before we left the restaurant. It continued through Saturday night, the entire next day and was still going strong at bedtime on Sunday night. Without knowing what I would wake up to the next morning, I set my alarm a little earlier to allow myself additional time to assess the situation — was it safe to drive and if so, how long would it take to shovel enough snow off the driveway to get my car out? — and to adjust myself accordingly — am I going to meet my client, or re-schedule?

Having done everything I could do to plan and prepare for whatever the morning would bring, I tucked myself into bed, turned out the light, said goodnight to my friend's cat and drifted peacefully off to sleep.

When my alarm went off Monday morning, I turned it off, laid back, enjoyed a long, delicious stretch, relaxed, and took stock of how I felt — pretty good! I smiled to myself, rolled onto my side to make eye contact with the cat and told her, "I would totally love a day off today, that would be so cool! And if that isn't how it pans out, I'm good. I totally got this, no matter what!"

The cat reached a paw out towards me and nudged her head onto my hand as if to say, "Ya, you do!" (Or maybe she just wanted a good ear rub?)

Either way, I got up out of bed, walked out to the living room window to see what was happening outside. It was slightly overcast and not very bright — the sun wasn't fully up yet. There was a bit of wind blowing already fallen snow around, but new snowfall had stopped. Looking at the end of the driveway I could tell snowplows had been out and even the residential side street I was on was reasonably clear, which meant I was going to go about my day as originally planned.

I went out and shovelled the driveway, cleared the snow off my car, shovelled that too, and came back inside. I enjoyed a nice hot shower, dressed, made a cup of tea and something to eat.

As I sat down to my breakfast, I checked my phone for messages.

There was one from my client: "Good morning Krista. Something has come up for me. Would it be okay for us to reschedule?"

MAGICAL!!!

Before replying, I paused to appreciate how, with Divine intervention I never could have anticipated, my manifestation of a day off had come to be. With a humbled ego and heart full of gratitude, I centred myself and said aloud, "Thank you for all my blessings, big and *small!*"

Krista Young - Yoga and Dance Instructor, Transformation Coach, Author

https://www.instagram.com/yourlife_take2/

https://www.facebook.com/krista.young.31105

In Memory Of Martin

Lauren Kinghorn

"Don't forget to pinch yourself," I say to our son. "Why?" he asks me. I answer with a giggle, "so you know it's real and not just a dream. It's something my Uncle Lionel taught me to do before my first overseas trip."

We had been dreaming about this moment for so long. Our son's first flight and his first trip to Durban to see his Dad's hometown. Daniel hadn't been back 'home' for 30 years.

And yet here we were, all three of us, safely buckled into our seats on a plane. Excited. Ready for take-off. And it all happened miraculously, out of the blue, like it was heaven sent.

A week before, we were preparing for our boy's first week back at school. That Friday morning, we received news that Martin, my husband's eldest brother, was about to go into surgery. Martin had been having dialysis three times a week for many years, and he was exhausted, body, mind and spirit.

We were not sure he would make it through the surgery, but he did. Martin called us on our family group chat that day, just after he had come out of surgery, saying he was tired. Ready to go. His heart gave in on Monday morning.

On Tuesday, our boy started Middle School, and we heard from Martin's eldest children that the memorial would take place that Saturday.

We started figuring out the money and logistics so Daniel could attend. Money was tight, especially that time of the year, January, after a month of holidays; and with all the back-to-school expenses.

By Tuesday afternoon, the miracles started pouring in. First, Daniel's company offered to pay for all three of our flights. What seemed impossible suddenly became possible. Then, a friend of Daniel's offered to drop off a car at the Durban airport for us to use while we were there.

We looked into accommodation and found a beautiful sea-facing apartment we could afford but the reviews said it was teeming with cockroaches. Another friend surprised us by calling to say he had booked us into a fancy resort in stunning Ballito Bay for the 3 days.

We were gobsmacked. Humbled by the incredible generosity and outpouring of love from Daniel's friends and colleagues.

The trip itself felt filled with magic and miracles too. We got to be with Daniel's family at this crucial, precious time and pay our respects to Martin. We got to see St. Martin's Home for Children where Daniel and his three brothers stayed after their parents passed away.

And, with no stress about finances, we got to experience some of Durban and the lush, tropical Dolphin Coast. Some beach time, fun in the waves, special family meals - time to connect and reminisce over delicious food, a mini holiday.

The highlight of our son's trip was the adrenaline rush of sliding down the highest slide in Africa, 'The Drop Zone' at Wet 'n Wild, the waterpark at uShaka Marine World. He did it three times. I wasn't that brave, but we had the best time together on the rest of the slides.

The highlight for me was an unexpected romantic moment on our first night at La Montagne. The gorgeous singer in the live band performed a pitch-perfect rendition of our wedding song, 'At Last' by Etta James. And suddenly, there I was again, walking downstairs in my wedding dress, tears in my eyes.

Our trip was both a sad farewell and the honeymoon we never had. This got me wondering. Were all these gifts and blessings from Martin himself? His spirit, his soul, his angelic self?

In every eulogy, Martin's family spoke of his kindness and generosity. Before he went in for his surgery, he paid for 6 months' rent in advance so his wife and the two girls would be safe and comfortable.

I looked up which Saint St. Martin's Home was named after. It was St. Martin of Tours, France.

The most famous story of St. Martin of Tours is about his generosity. While he was still a soldier in the French army, he took pity on a beggar. He cut his cloak in half to share it with the beggar to prevent him from freezing to death during the night. During the night, he dreamed that Jesus introduced him to his disciples, saying, "this is my friend, Martin, who shared his cloak with me". When he awoke, the beggar was gone and the cloak was back in one piece.

I like to think that our Martin, too, is in Heaven now, happily back in one piece, reunited with his parents, his first wife who died many years ago and their son who died 5 years ago.

I imagine Martin happy, healthy, whole, relaxed, and beaming, as I thank him for these precious memories.

Lauren Kinghorn - Transformation Life Coach & Energy Healer

https://laurenkinghorn.com/miracles

https://laurenkinghorn.com/book-now

A Final Goodbye

Leila Garde

I was a young twenty-two year old, naïve and self-absorbed; when news arrived at my front door one Sunday morning at around ten o'clock. My beloved brother had passed. My parents couldn't get hold of me as - my mobile phone was off; and as I lived in a different city, they had sent friends of theirs to knock at my door. I remember it as a brief visitation that changed my life in a single moment, fraught with disbelief and confusion. My brother of twenty-nine, healthy, fit, and in the prime of his life, with literally *everything* to live for, had been ripped away from my world.

07 July 1996... nearly thirty years ago and I remember it as if it were yesterday.

I recall sitting perched on the end of my couch, the only piece of furniture I owned at the time, hearing that there had been some sort of accident. My young mind was ill-prepared to learn that the very man I had admired and looked up to my entire life had taken his own with a single self-inflicted gunshot to the head. Even today I battle to find the words to express the shock and immense grief that no human should ever have the need to bear.

I flew home that afternoon, arriving at dusk. The sky was a pale indigo and I noticed the luminous crescent moon hanging overhead. Venus, the evening star, shimmered brightly alongside it. I felt as if this was his wonderous way of letting us know that he was okay....that he was somehow nearby....and that he was sorry. And so, the moon became my forever guardian and throughout my life I would - and still do - randomly look up at the night sky to find that same celestial alignment and feel instantly that our souls were still connected.

That night, my sister and I chose to sleep together. No one should sleep alone when enveloped by such grief. The air was cool and the shadows of the garden outside danced beyond the windows, veiled by the pale green curtains. We lay awake late into the night talking and remembering. Mom and Dad had gone to bed early. Medicated I was told. The old house creaked as the cold winter air set in; the wooden rafters groaned like bone cracking in the dark, sharp and wet, the sound echoing through the empty hallways. But then there came a stillness. We paused in conversation, and as our breathing slowed the air seemed to birth a ball of light that hovered above us. Fine static energy, much like an untuned television hung in the dark; and then it flattened itself over us as if to give us a hug - the energy momentarily thrumming through our bodies, warm and loving. And then, as quickly as he had arrived, he was gone. He was truly gone!

When asked to write on miracles, this is the first one that comes to mind - though of course there have been many more throughout my life. Even on the drive home from his funeral, our car had become trapped between a sixteen-wheeler and another truck as we merged onto the highway. I was certain we would die. Yet somehow, although I cannot recall how, the vehicles and us with them, miraculously passed through that moment without harm, as if lifted, rearranged and set down again by unseen hands.

The weeks and months that followed Greg's death were blurred. Everything appeared and sounded different. Muffled... not quite real, except for the grief of course. The grief remained alive and tangible, set deep behind my ribs for years to come. But with time and with the passing of every anniversary, the pain did eventually begin to ease. I learned to smile and laugh again. And much later, I found the teacher in the grief: I learned gratitude for life; I learned to be less self-aware and more connected to others; I learned to appreciate the everyday miracles.... eating fruit in the sunshine, spreading my toes through the sand, enjoying a miraculous sunset, and admiring a super full moon. I suppose not all miracles are about roses and rainbows; some come with hard lessons attached - lessons that shape and mold our being, throwing us deeper into the human experience; waiting, watching to see what becomes of us. Remembering now this miracle, his visitation and his final good-bye takes me right back. It's an embittered memory rich in paradox, one that leaves me feeling both so blessed and yet still so filled with sadness. But no doubt, next time I look up at the night sky, I will find him there, gazing down upon his little sister, reminding her to find the miracles and the beauty in all that exists! Reminding all, including you, to keep shining on!

Leila Garde - Artist and Life Coach

https://www.instagram.com/leila.garde.art/

https://www.facebook.com/leila.garde.9

Touched By An Angel

Leslie Ellis

In each and every moment of our lives there are potential miracles just waiting to be activated.

Sometimes, in the most unanticipated way, your life can completely turn around.

My life has been dedicated to service. I help women to value themselves and to move through the anxiety, overwhelm, and resentment that keeps them disconnected from the vast meaning that their lives could have.

In my younger days, I was already disconnected. I had no sense of meaning and little sense that I had anything to give.

And then I met Jerry.

My car wouldn't start one morning, so I was going to have to ride the bus to work.

It figured. That morning everything seemed to be going to shit. I felt awful. I was anxious and really unhappy.

I didn't know how I was going to make it through the day at my job on a locked, adult, psychiatric unit. I wondered again, "Who will notice? And will they take my keys and make me stay there, where I probably belong – as a patient?"

Therapy was getting me by but even as I waited for my counselor to be ready for our sessions, I would stand at the top of the stairwell and think how easy, and what a relief, it would be to just drop over the rail.

I never made a suicide attempt but the images and plans consumed my mind much of the time. I was actively trying to feel "better" but I couldn't imagine not having these thoughts. They were so much a part of my experience of each day that there didn't seem to be a world in which I could live...and not think constantly about dying.

A place where I wanted to be alive wasn't a place I could envision. I didn't see any vision for a "future me". And I certainly didn't have a roadmap for getting there.

That day, 35 years ago, is burned into my memory.

It's a day that completely changed the trajectory of my life. The day I met Jerry.

I was there, at the bus stop, feeling the pressures of the world on my shoulders, wondering how I was going to make it through the day, trying to bolster myself up so that I could do my job and help the patients in my care - the ones who didn't see any value in living or who were so disconnected from "reality" that a meaning filled life seemed out of reach.

I empathized with them. But I had to hide it. No one could know how bad I felt or my world might really fall apart completely.

I saw the bus coming down the street and as I started to walk toward the place where the doors would open and I'd have to step into another day of pretend... a tall, thin, African American man walked up beside me and said "Hi". He had an afro, and was wearing bell bottom pants, a colorful shirt and a vest. He looked like he'd stepped straight out of the 1970's.

I smiled, returned his greeting and looked down, determined not to engage.

He was right behind me as we mounted the steps into the very full, standing-room only bus. We stopped about halfway down the aisle, where we were destined to try to stay upright as the bus lurched forward, then stopped and started over and over again all the way to downtown.

"I'm Jerry.", he said with a grin, as if I cared. And he proceeded to tell me about what he was going to do that day and asked me questions to which I delivered short, curt, but polite responses.

Undeterred, he kept up a light banter throughout the entire trip. It was the kind of conversation that was basically benign, a little annoying, and completely forgettable. Until the bus reached my stop and I was nudging past Jerry to get off...

He said to me, "It was nice talking to you Leslie." Then he lightly touched me on the arm and said, "Isn't it a great day to be alive?"

And in that instant something changed inside of me.

I couldn't tell you exactly what it was or just how it happened, but I felt different. My step was a little lighter as I made my way to transfer to the next bus.

My day at work was as usual except that I didn't feel like I was hiding the fact that I felt like I was going to cry all day.

I kept thinking about Jerry. And I was convinced that he was an angel in disguise. He was there, that morning, to help me to see something I hadn't seen for a very long time.

There was a way forward for me.

It was a great day to be alive. And I wanted to live.

And so I have. Lived. I've lived with purpose and with meaning and I now ask you: what difference would it make in your life if you were fully living, as you?

Leslie Ellis – Yoga Therapist and Soul Embodiment Coach

https://yogaheartsong.com

https://www.facebook.com/leslie.ellis.359

The Miracle Didn't Arrive Wrapped In Beauty Or Celebration

Leslie Klatt

Nobody showed up at my front door with an oversized check and a camera crew. It didn't come with balloons or applause or relief. It arrived quietly, suddenly and without my permission. It arrived as pain. The kind of pain that stops you in your tracks whether you are ready or not.

I was bedridden for over a month; a month and a half, really. I couldn't hold my head up, I couldn't walk. I could crawl, I could roll, I could lie still. That was it. I ended up in the hospital for days, confused and frightened by how quickly my body had shut everything down.

I have a high pain tolerance. I birthed three children at home without medication. I'm not someone who gets sick easily and I am not someone who stops. But this stopped me completely.

And it came at the worst possible time.

I am a single mom with three kids. I had just moved into a house that was a stretch to afford. I was responsible for everything and I was preparing for a court battle with my ex who made my life a living hell.

Lying in bed for 6 weeks isn't exactly encouraged at this point in life.
But the Universe knew better.

Before that moment, I had been working relentlessly towards the life that I wanted for myself and for my children. I was building... planning, pushing, aligning myself over and over again with goals that looked right on paper. Income goals, client goals, business models that made sense intellectually, paths that other people had proven successful.

I kept telling myself to go all in and to refine, to push through resistance, to trust that effort would eventually get me the results. But what I was building didn't actually ever get me there.

And left uninterrupted, I would have repeated the same pattern again... another structure that required me to override myself - and probably dating another dodo.

Enter divine intervention... the miracle.

Looking back, I now know that I was given more pleasant signs that my efforts were going along the wrong path. But I ignored them. I tried harder. The signs got louder and my efforts became fiercer. This time, the intervention made sure I heard it.
It stopped me. I thought I was going to die.

When your body takes away your ability to move, to work, to think clearly, to manage everything and everyone else, it forces an honesty that ambition alone will never force.

There was no pushing through this.
The more I couldn't hustle, the more stressed out I got and the more I saw my business slip away.

I had to be still. And I don't recall the last time I was ever still.

And in that stillness, everything reorganized itself.

When I started to come out of it, it was as clear as day that the trajectory I was on would never deliver the experience I wanted for myself or for my children.

That interruption, the divine intervention... unwanted, inconvenient, terrifying... became the pivot point.

Once I was able to move again, nothing went back to how it had been.

My life didn't magically become easier, but it became clearer.
The noise fell away. The 'forcing' stopped; what fit became obvious; what didn't became impossible to justify.

My personal goals aligned. My children stabilized, their confidence grew, their peace grew and my income returned. Not through the version of work I thought I had to do, but through the work I had always been built for.

I stopped forcing business models that required constant emotional labor. I stopped trying to sell work that confused people. I stopped shrinking the skills I had spent decades refining. I have always been excellent at execution, at operations, at logistics, at planning, systems, marketing and growth. I can walk into a business and improve it quickly, not with hype, but with structure; not with motivation, but with clarity.

What changed wasn't my capability.
What changed was alignment.

That experience taught me something that I carry with me now: miracles don't always show up to give you what you want:
Sometimes they show up to take away what's blocking it.
Sometimes they look like consequences.

Sometimes they look like loss.
Sometimes they look like being stopped when you least want to be.

But when they arrive (and they always arrive), you still end up having the experience you were reaching for - just not the way you imagined.

Miracles present opportunities, not outcomes. The opportunity might be to stop, to pivot, to rebuild, to redesign your life and business so they can actually hold what you're asking for.

Being forced to get clarity means you can recognize when something is for you and when it isn't especially when external circumstances are pulling at you, testing your boundaries, trying to draft you into stories that aren't yours.

When your life is built with intention, interruptions don't derail you, they redirect you. They accelerate you toward the path you would have found eventually if you had been willing to stop sooner, instead of pushing harder. You would have recognized the 'stop' signs never turned to 'go' signs.

That was my miracle.

Big, painful, scary, mysterious, out of nowhere, complete intervention that didn't allow me to push through. It forced the change that was needed. It realigned me with what I was meant to do to achieve the goals I was always pursuing.

And once you know how to recognize them, you start to see them everywhere.

Leslie Klatt - Business Operations and Project Management Pro

www.opshaus.ca

www.leslieklatt.com

Two Beating Hearts

Lisa Doucette

Miracles are normal and I have the joy of waking up to mine every single day. My twins are living, breathing proof that the Universe is always listening. All we have to do is ask, believe and then... surrender.

I have always been a late bloomer; late to school, late to puberty, late to love. I was 36 when I finally felt secure enough—financially, emotionally, spiritually—to begin trying for a family. Like so many women, I assumed it would happen naturally. But months passed. Then years. Nothing.

We turned to a fertility clinic and went through every test imaginable...bloodwork, ultrasounds, hormone panels... the works. The result? "Unexplained infertility." They told me I had a 1% chance of conceiving naturally. One percent! My heart shattered. I had always imagined myself as a mother. I could almost see the children in my dreams. But those dreams now felt so far away...like someone else's life.

We were financially stretched at the time. My husband had just immigrated and we were rebuilding from scratch. Fertility treatments weren't covered by our Provincial health care and IVF carried a massive price tag of between $15,000 and $20,000 with only a 40% success rate. It felt like we were gambling our life savings on a maybe.

Thus we opted for a more modest option — Controlled Ovarian Hyperstimulation (COH) — which involved daily medications, ultrasounds, bloodwork and a much smaller price tag. But with all of that came lower odds. Only a 10% chance of success.

We had managed to save enough to try two rounds. I prayed that the first one would work. During that cycle, my body responded quickly. But at one point I had four follicles, which meant they might cancel the round altogether due to too high a risk of multiples. The next day, one follicle slowed down, leaving three. Then two. We were cleared to proceed.

That Sunday, I went to church. Although I don't attend regularly anymore, I grew up Catholic and being in the sanctuary felt like slipping into a warm bath of memory and comfort. That morning, the priest spoke about the power of prayer and something he said shifted everything: "When you pray, don't just ask. Thank God as if the prayer has already been answered." I clung to that. I decided right then and there, that I would act in gratitude, as if I was already pregnant.

On my way home from church, I stopped at a department store and bought a tiny bib that read *World's Best Poppy*. I pictured my dad's face when I gave it to him. In my heart, I was already expecting.

The morning of the procedure, I visualized a tiny embryo forming, a spark of light finding its home within me. Over the next two weeks, I whispered to my belly every morning: *You are safe. You are loved. You are already here.*

Then came the phone call. I was at work when I answered the phone, hands trembling. "You're pregnant!" My due date was November 13th.
My heart soared.

But just a few days later, I started bleeding. I rushed to the ER, terrified. After hours of waiting, I was told, bluntly, that one-third of pregnancies end in miscarriage and that I wasn't far enough along to see anything on an ultrasound. "You can try again," they said.

I was gutted.

They scheduled follow-up bloodwork. My HCG levels were still rising but not doubling the way they were supposed to. My doctor ordered an early ultrasound at 7 weeks. I braced myself for the worst.

The technician was kind. I explained everything—fertility treatments, the bleed, the anxiety. She scanned quietly for a few moments, then turned the screen toward me. There, flickering like a star in the night, was a perfectly strong heartbeat.

I burst into tears. It was the most beautiful thing I had ever seen. She assured me everything looked good.

Then she paused. "How many embryos did they transfer?" "None," I said, laughing nervously. "We didn't do IVF."

I asked her if she saw something else on the screen. She squinted at the screen, then zoomed in.

Another heartbeat. Twins! From two follicles, two miracles had been born. My babies. My double blessing.

Today, those babies are 11 years old... bright, beautiful souls who call me Mom. And every time I look into their eyes, I remember that Sunday in church, the whispered prayers, the terrifying wait and the moment those heartbeats danced on that screen.

Miracles aren't always big, flashy or loud. Sometimes, they arrive gently, in their own time, tucked within the quiet corners of hope.

And sometimes, they show up as two tiny heartbeats — against all odds and in perfect time.

Life has handed me my share of challenges, but one thing I've learned is this: miracles happen every single day when we have faith and surrender. When we shift our focus, we shift our reality. The birth of my twins is living proof of that.

Today, I am not only their mom, but also the owner of a small business dedicated to helping women discover the faith within themselves, align with the seasons and tap into their own magic. Miracles may not be perfect, but they are always abundant – especially when you show up for yourself.

Through my business, Crooked Crown of Gems, I help women move from overwhelm and disconnection into clarity, confidence, and deep self-trust. I am a Reiki Master and Teacher, death doula, Human Design guide, and women's circle facilitator, offering a blend of energy work, intuitive insight, and nature-based practices to support women through healing, transition, and transformation.

Lisa Doucette - Reiki Master & Teacher, Death Doula, Human Design Guide
www.crookedcrownofgems.ca
https://www.instagram.com/crookedcrownofgems/

Hurricane Drama Momma

Loria Raiola

"You have twenty minutes to get in the car! We're evacuating!"

"NO Mom!! I want to stay home!" protested my son Daniel.

"You do NOT have a choice! We are going to the shelter and taking Shiva & Boots with us!"

"I'm not going!" shouted Jermain, Danny's twin brother.

"You heard your mother," said their father. Get your sleeping bag and put it in the car. Hurry up!!"

"But we stayed home last hurricane...", pleaded Jermain, trying his best to negotiate.

"This one is different, Jey. It's coming at us at a possible category 5 and we're NOT taking any chances, so let's get going!"

"Ugh!" they replied in unison... and within twenty minutes we arrived six miles inland at the local elementary school, now a shelter for those evacuating from Hurricane Milton.

The day before our evacuation, Milton's trajectory had made an abrupt shift in course. Now the storm was forecast to make a direct hit over Siesta Key, (about 4.5 miles from our house) and land as a category 4 hurricane or perhaps a 5, as some news stations predicted. This sobering news was not good and the potential for catastrophic damage was all too real.

What I did not know was that FEMA trucks, equipped with hundreds of body bags had arrived and were parked behind Sarasota Memorial Hospital just waiting.

I was glad that I had listened to my guidance that morning and I was not taking any chances. The shelter was brick and looked sturdy, but the entrance had a lot of glass windows and doors. I pondered what if?

As the hours went by, we received texts, messages and phone calls from family and friends, many of whom I had not spoken to in years, triggering an array of feelings!

The entire world was watching this storm. It was predicted to be the storm of the century and now it had arrived!

A few days before, I had participated in a special vigil with the global organization Connecting Consciousness. The consensus was that this was no ordinary event but that we as a collective were not powerless. We prayed together. We sent love to Milton. We forgave Milton. We encouraged Milton to express in a way that would not be all that destructive over the land. We invoked God, Mother Earth, Archangel Michael and our guardian angels.

Later on, I found out that many individuals, shamans and spiritual groups were praying and holding vigils all over the state, region and globe for this one event, forming a planetary Team of Light. I believe that this global unified field of consciousness dissolved Milton from a category 5 to a category 3.

Getting back to the shelter... it was approaching 4:00pm and the conditions outside were continuing to deteriorate when my phone rang. It was my friend John.

“Loria, where are you?”

"We’re at the shelter John.”

“In Sarasota?”

“Yes.”

“GET OUT OF THERE!!!”

"John, we’re OK. We’re about 6 miles inland.”

“Six miles? OK, but I just want you to be prepared for what you are going to see when you get out.”

I was listening....

“You’re going to see a lot of destruction and dead bodies floating, so be prepared.”

This was something I was not prepared to see I thought, as my stomach flinched.

“John, a bunch of us prayed before the storm, so it’s going to be OK.” I was trying to keep calm.

“I know kiddo, you’re strong. And they’re going to need you.”

“I think we’re safe here John. I’m not worried.”

“OK, I just want you to know that I love you.”

"Thank you, John I appreciate your call, love you too."

I suddenly felt sick to my stomach and began to hyperventilate. I soothed myself by deepening my breath and slowing it down.

By 4:00 am the eye had passed and we were allowed to leave the shelter. Cautiously we waited for the sun to rise and proceeded home. There were downed trees and many homes had roof damage, but nothing like they had predicted. Some folks on the coast experienced major flooding. At the end of the day four lives were lost throughout the state in car accidents. Fortunately, no one in our area died. We made it and so did our neighbors and friends! Yay!

For almost a year however, after the storm, I was experiencing PTSD. This trauma clouded my perception and triggered unhealthy stress in my body, emotions and mind. I finally came to terms with my anxiety by using my spiritual tools daily and consistently. I was not going to live traumatized anymore!

Today I am more grateful than ever before. I can see the gift in almost every experience, trauma and situation.

My life is a gift!

Milton taught me to navigate the world with greater confidence and strength. And for that I AM grateful.

Angel Yogi Loria Ra (Loria Raiola) - Spiritual Psychotherapist, Award-Winning Author, Wellness Professional in the Healing Arts.

https://liveyounger.com/ridingthewave

lorianow@gmail.com

Refusal To Give Up: The Miracle Of Believing And Showing Up

Maria Victoria Cabalu

This chapter is dedicated to those who keep going when they feel exhausted, or those who continue to move forward when the path is unclear. If you are still standing, still hoping, still showing up even if you're tired and overwhelmed, it is a powerful declaration of your strength and faith.

We are often conditioned to look for miracles in the grand, the extraordinary, the sudden breakthroughs, the dramatic rescue... but there are also miracles that are quieter and more subtle because belief doesn't always roar back like a blazing fire. Sometimes it returns as a whisper, or a fragile flicker after the storm. When you've been through the hurt, the doubt and the silence, and you still choose to believe again? That's miraculous!

They are the quiet moments when something inside you refuses to give up; like getting out of bed when it's easier to put things off; making the call when you feel like you have nothing left; taking one small step forward when everything inside you says, "what's the point?"

Through the cracks of broken moments, after everything has been torn apart, the steady presence of belief is what shines through the gaps and refuses to be ignored. I recall the time when my son's health took a downward spiral. I remember those painstaking moments of taking my son from doctor to doctor, to and from clinics and ER, desperate for answers. My heart sank as I watched him grow weaker, struggling with fatigue and shortness of breath. As a mother, It was hard to bear. I felt powerless not being able to get the help my son needed, especially knowing deep down that something wasn't right. In desperation, I cried in silence asking God for guidance.

Weeks after what felt like an endless cycle of disappointment, my prayers were answered! The next doctor we found didn't waste any time in his assessment and he proceeded to drain out cloudy fluid from an area that had previously been dismissed as nothing more than muscle tension. My son was urgently admitted into hospital, with results confirming that it was a serious life-threatening infection and dangerously close to his spine. We focused on his healing and on his continued ability to walk, with a very grateful heart.

Due to the doctor's experience and quick assessment, my son was admitted into the isolation unit and he finally received the treatment he needed. The long hours wearing the mask were unbearable for me as days turned into nights and vice versa. However, this was nothing compared to what would have been worse, had my son lost hope. Days turned into weeks, and each day that he was able to endure the treatments was a miracle. Filling him with love, encouragement and support was my mission to ensure that he would keep strong and continue to believe in his healing despite what he was going through. It was important that he could draw upon the belief and the strength of others around him. I chose to be a strong advocate for his care and in keeping him hopeful.

The subtle but powerful act of deciding that we're not done, that we're still capable and that tomorrow holds the possibility of something better, is a choice. To choose faith over fear, hope over despair, and taking actions that matter are daily miracles. I believe that when you make this kind of choice, it transforms not just your life, but the world around you.

The truth is, sometimes showing up doesn't always feel miraculous. Some days it feels like you're dragging yourself through fog. There's resistance, fear, doubt... But by choosing to act, even when you're afraid, you are stepping into alignment with something divine.

When you believe and show up, your impact and the light that you are, expand, creating a ripple effect. It is incredibly profound when someone who is watching you says, "if she can do it, maybe I can too."

Your courage becomes contagious. Your belief becomes a light. And even if you never hear the full story of how you have impacted someone's life, know this: **nothing done with love, truth and bold belief is ever wasted.**

Choosing to show up can change your path, make a difference, create miracles that happen every day.

My son's journey was nothing short of miraculous, from every courageous choice to the belief that turned despair into hope, and darkness into healing. It was a testament of refusing to give up even when the odds are stacked against you, and you rising through it all, are living proof of that power.

The smallest act of showing up again and again, turns belief into becoming. That's where the tide turns. That's where the impossible starts to shift. That's where you remember: you were never powerless because you are the miracle in motion!

"Never underestimate the power of your presence because even the smallest light can shine through the darkest night." — *Maria Victoria Cabalu*

Maria Victoria Cabalu - Coach, Speaker, Author
https://www.facebook.com/MariaVictoriaCabalu
MariaVictoriaCabalu.co

A Father's Dream, A Daughter's Miracle

Marina Vucurevic

In May 2002, my father passed away. Years earlier, when I left Germany to move to South Africa in 1997, he shared something unusual with me. He told me that he had been dreaming of a black hand. Until then, he had never spoken to me about his dreams. At the time, neither of us understood what it meant.

For most of my adult life, I was single. I was drawn to men who were unavailable, often much older than me and I felt no desire to marry or to have children — ever. Only much later would I understand why this was, but that is another story.

During the final year and a half of my father's life, I commuted between South Africa and Germany to be with him. After he passed, I returned to Cape Town in October 2002, emotionally depleted but ready to rebuild my life. One evening, while catching up with a man I had been involved with before returning to Germany, I suddenly heard myself say, "I want to start a family." The words came out unplanned and unexpected. It was immediately clear that I didn't mean to do this with him, but the moment felt like a declaration to the Universe and one that surprised us both.

What I didn't yet know was that, within weeks, life would answer.

I have always had a quiet gift for connecting people. Several close friends met their life partners through me, not by design but by following my intuition. This time, it seemed that the invisible hand of fate was working on my behalf.

I ran into an old acquaintance and we decided to meet a few days later as I was planning to go away for the weekend. Unbeknownst to me, during those few days he had met a stranger visiting from the UK in a bookshop at the Waterfront. He took him under his wing, showing him Cape Town and taking him along wherever he went. That stranger was Chris, a black man from the UK who had come to Cape Town for a short stay before moving on to New York.

Our meeting turned into an evening beach picnic at one of Cape Town's iconic Clifton beaches. My acquaintance mentioned that he would be bringing two friends. The moment they arrived, Chris and I looked at each other and something unmistakable passed between us. It was love at first sight, immediate and undeniable.

We sat in the sand surrounded by candlelit picnics; the evening feeling suspended in time. I didn't want the night to end. Neither did Chris.

We didn't exchange phone numbers and I had to rely on my acquaintance to reconnect us. When the long-awaited call finally came, he asked to see me and invited me to a Russian ballet performed outdoors at one of Cape Town's romantic wine estates. Our first date unfolded as if perfectly orchestrated.

It was magical. We both knew that something profound had begun.

The weeks that followed were filled with joy and ease. We spent nearly every moment together as I showed him my beloved Cape Town. When my birthday arrived in early December, I told friends and family that I was in love and that this time was different. Understandably, many were cautious. Even I was still catching my breath.

Chris had arrived in Cape Town in November 2002 intending to stay only briefly before moving on to New York. Instead, he never left. He is still here with me now, in 2026.

From the beginning, he felt guided to buy property. I showed him a charming apartment in Sea Point that I had once stayed in and loved. Less than four weeks after we met, he bought the flat. It became and still is my dream home, in a place that continues to feel deeply blessed.

A few months later, we spoke about starting a family. And against all expectations, in 2006, just weeks before my 43rd birthday, I gave birth to a beautiful baby boy.

Only then did I fully understand my father's dream.

The black hand had been a promise, a symbol of what was to come. I found true happiness at the age of 38, less than six months after my father had crossed over. Perhaps because, in some mysterious way, he was helping me from beyond, guiding me gently toward my miracle.

Marina Vucurevic - Storyteller & Life Enthusiast
https://www.facebook.com/marina.vucurevic.7
https://www.linkedin.com/in/marina-vucurevic-101b322ab/

Starting Over

Melanie Basson

The finalization of my divorce in late August 1995 followed a brutally cold winter, perhaps intensified by the emotional turmoil of a difficult year. At under 30, I suddenly found myself a single mother to two wonderful little boys, then aged seven and four. The subsequent loss of my Dad in April 1996 left my Mom alone in their 3-bedroom house, compounding the grief for me and my two children.

Yet, through this hardship, a blessing emerged: God's wisdom brought us together. My Mom and I moved in with each other, providing mutual support through a very tough time and crucially, offering stability for my sons. They adored their Gran and the arrangement seemed perfect for everyone.

We eventually established a routine and tried to make the best of our new life, though the lingering heartache and disappointment remained. One sunny afternoon, my Mom came into the living room with an unfamiliar look on her face. "What's wrong?" I asked.

"I think we should move closer to your brother," she said. "This house is a constant reminder of loss and it's making me depressed. I believe a new start would do us all good — you, me and the boys."

We agreed immediately. The next morning, she contacted my brother. After a long conversation, they too came to an agreement. She put the house on the market and by God's grace, it sold quickly. We packed our belongings in record time, albeit with mixed emotions. My ex-husband came by to say goodbye to the boys and it was much harder for him than I had anticipated. Seeing the clear sadness in his eyes, I regretted that he had to ache so much, despite our divorce.

The moving truck left ahead of us. With only one car, my Mom drove for three hours while I looked after the children and our Jack Russell, Cindy. We arrived at the 'new' house just as the sun was setting. Exhausted but excited, everyone piled out, clutching as many blankets and pillows as they could carry. We set up a giant bed in the living room, ate sandwiches and drank juice and were fast asleep by 9:00 PM.

My brother visited the following morning with excellent news: as the manager of a gas and outdoor shop, he offered me a job as a cashier. I accepted instantly. My Mom agreed to look after the boys until they could be enrolled in the nearest school. Things were finally looking up and I was eager to start.

On day three, my Mom called me around lunchtime. She said my youngest had developed the flu and that she had given him some medication from her old medicine box. She assured me that she would keep an eye on him and that he was resting in bed. His older brother, she reported, was outside playing with the dog and seemed to be adapting well.

However, she called again at four o'clock. My brother, looking pale, emerged from his office and (since we weren't allowed cellphones while working) relayed the message: my youngest son was missing! My Mom had been frantically searching for three hours. New to the neighborhood, she had desperately hoped to find him before I came home.

I went numb and began to cry uncontrollably. The gas-delivery driver, witnessing my distress, offered his immediate and immense sympathy. We sprinted to his vehicle and he drove me home in a reckless twenty minutes, doing some 'low flying.' I leaped out, ran inside and screamed his name, completely overwhelmed. I reached the hallway and stood frozen. Fifty, horrific scenarios flashed through my mind, including the green, leaf-covered pool next door. My heart shattered at the thought of a tragic outcome.

In that very moment, a shift in the air, a movement almost imperceptible, caught my eye. He slid out from underneath the dining table that had been draped with a tablecloth. The surrounding chairs, pushed carelessly in after the last meal, had formed a makeshift fort, obscuring him completely from my mother's desperate view. For hours, she had been frantic, a whirlwind of worry and fear, her voice hoarse from calling his name.

The high fever, a relentless heat that had flushed his cheeks earlier that day, had driven him to seek that cool, dark sanctuary. There, tucked away in the silence, he had finally fallen into a deep, fever-induced sleep, a slumber so profound it had sealed him off from the anxiety raging just feet away.

It was only later, after the initial, dizzying relief had subsided, that we discovered that he had an ear infection which contributed to him not hearing her either. The combination of fever and pain had orchestrated his accidental, terrifying disappearance.

I froze; a sudden, blinding recognition replacing the darkness. My knees buckled and I knelt on the hallway floor, a soundless plea escaping. Still groggy, his eyes widened with confused relief and he ran straight into my arms. The physical impact grounded me, dissolving the panic into an overwhelming reality of him pressed against me. Holding his small, trembling body, smelling the faint scent of fever and sleep was the most profound, sacred moment of my life. The world was finally right.

Melanie Basson – Professional Caregiver

https://www.instagram.com/basson6309/

Walking Away From The Wreck

Melissa Steffy

I still think of it sometimes, how ordinary that day looked before everything turned around. One moment I was driving, and the next I was staring at a big white truck barreling toward me with no sign of slowing down. There was no space to move, no path on which to escape, only that split second where I understood exactly what was coming... and then chaos! Metal twisting... glass breaking with that sharp, sickening pop... the world spinning like a front-loading washer on full tilt. In the middle of all of it, the only thing left to do was to surrender enough to protect whatever I could.

Then silence. The kind that feels wrong, as if the world had hit pause. My truck lay upside down in a ditch and I was hanging from my seatbelt, breath ragged, heart pounding in my ears. Blood rushing to my head, I registered one truth: I'm still here. Suspended above broken glass and crushed metal, I was still alive.

The miracle didn't arrive with trumpets or beams of light. It was in how the truck had landed. Upside down, yes, but somehow tucked into the ditch in this unlikely way where the cab was the only part not destroyed. A nearby Ring camera caught the accident, and even watching it later, it looked surreal. Balanced just right so that I could unclip myself, I crawled out and stood on solid earth again.

Strangers appeared almost immediately. They had been behind me and saw the whole thing. Their voices come back to me more clearly than their faces do. The Yorkshire woman whose hands shook as she tried to steady me; the way they guided me into their truck, asking if I could breathe, if anything felt wrong, waiting with me until the ambulance arrived. I don't remember their names, but I do remember the way their kindness wrapped around me when everything else felt surreal.

Walking away felt like a triumph. Proof that I had outrun the worst of it. I told myself that the miracle was complete. What I didn't understand was that my body still held chapters that I hadn't read yet.

The scar across my clavicle became a permanent reminder of the seatbelt that saved my life. My neck was wrecked and demanded years of treatment. The hidden damage in my hip stayed quiet at first, revealing itself only slowly. My concussion wasn't identified until three days later, and when everything finally settled, the pain was brutal.

Some things healed over time. Others became louder. Migraines that clamped down for weeks turned into years of work retraining my eyes so they would cooperate again. On the outside, life had moved on. Inside, I was still living inside the impact.

Then came January 2024. I fell. That fall forced the unseen into view. After trying everything else, the orthopedist finally said the words that changed the whole story: the head of my femur was damaged beyond repair. My hip joint had been deteriorating since the crash. The replacement surgery in September 2024 shifted everything and by the end of January 2025, I could finally put down the pain medication I had depended on for almost eight years.

Surviving the wreck hadn't closed the chapter. My body kept speaking and the pain shaped my days, asking for attention I did not want to give. I was furious that gratitude for surviving was not enough to erase the ache. I believed that walking away should have been the end. But pain doesn't follow neat narrative arcs... it travels with you. It slips into your choices, your sleep, the quiet corners of your life.

Eventually I understood that the miracle wasn't only in climbing out of an upside-down truck, it was in what the long road afterward carved into me. Patience. Slowness. A different kind of listening. Compassion for my own limits. Once you've hung upside down from a seatbelt and realized you're still alive, you develop a sense for the suffering that others carry. You notice it sooner. You honor it.

The miracle lived in those strangers who steadied me. It lived in the resilience I found when pain refused to let me look away. I walked out of that ditch convinced I had slipped past death and in a way, I did. But what I see now is that the miracle kept unfolding through recovery, through surgery and through the stubborn work of becoming someone more present, more awake, more alive.

Survival was the beginning. Growth became the real miracle. And every day since then, no matter the ache, I have kept walking. That counts as a miracle too.

Melissa Steffy - Systems Creator, Writer, and Sovereign Living Architect

https://www.facebook.com/miss.allowing

https://www.facebook.com/groups/techwhisperermel

Full Circle

Merryl Seibert

I made a quick trip to Vegas for 2 days and Tasha, my furry daughter, stayed with my then fiancé. He always called to say goodnight at midnight. I came into my hotel room seeing a message light blinking. How sweet I thought, my goodnight message.

I listened and got the shock of a lifetime. I dropped the phone and fell to the floor crying hysterically. My world stopped. He said, "Tasha's Dead".

Nothing else. No hello. No goodnight. No sorry. No explanation! He knew she was my furry daughter and not just a dog. And all he said in a message was, "Tasha's dead."

Although Miracles happen all the time, this one took 30 years to appear...

I came back from that trip in shock and my life was never the same again.

As I was a Hollywood Mystic at the time, Tasha was my conduit and she channeled information telepathically for me to share with clients. After the initial information of her demise, I psychically connected with her and asked her if her soul would ever come back to me?

She said that I would know it was her when I found "a little white dog with paw prints that looked like upside down hearts on her back".

Wow! She gave me such detail and I thanked her.

Although I felt devastated and depressed, I still continued to work as the Hollywood Mystic but I did not have Tasha as my conduit. While still grieving deeply, I began going to shelters looking for the white dog with beige paw prints on her back, but to no avail.

Having felt remorse, my fiancé got me 2 puppies. One was white - no spots and one was brindle and white, and I grew to love them dearly but Tasha did not make an appearance.

15 years passed and I rescued 3 Chihuahuas. I forgot about Tasha's message.

Then one of my Chihuahua's, Shadow, passed during the pandemic of 2020. The second one, Blacky, passed in 2022 and the last of that family, Coco, passed in 2024 at almost 17 years old.

I remembered asking a Pet Psychic if Tasha visits through my dogs and she said, "No, she will come back to me in my next dog." I laughed and said, "there's not going to be a next one. These are my last!"

Months later, I was feeling depressed and unmotivated to work or to do much of anything after my last dog, Coco, had passed.

I once again attempted to look in shelters to rescue a new pet.

There was a little white Chihuahua who had come in as a stray. I went to see her and she was aloof, looking beyond all the people as if she was only looking for her owner. She didn't wag her tail or give kisses. Instead she was fearful, trembling with her tail between her legs.

I immediately adopted her and we went home. She had just been spayed and had a cone around her neck and was wrapped in a blanket. I let her stay snuggled for a while till she adjusted to her new environment. Lo and behold… when I removed the blanket and cone, I got goosebumps down my spine…here was the "little white dog with 2 beige paw prints on her back" that Tasha said I would know it was her returning back to me. Through reincarnation, I feel she is reunited with me and back home again.

Miracles can happen even 30 years later!

Currently, I am an Intuitive Life And Energy Coach. I use Quantum Energy Frequencies to balance energy, Chakras and Meridians in people and in pets. Occasionally, I go to shelters to calm the ones who have anxiety so that they have a better chance at being adopted.

I believe that Tasha is reincarnated and came back to me as my shelter dog I adopted, named Chloe. My Little White Chihuahua Shelter dog has her own Instagram page called The_Chi_Squad: From Shelter Stray to Chloe, the Spoiled Chi-va! Check her out.

Merryl Seibert - Intuitive Life and Energy Coach
https://www.facebook.com/merryl.seibert
https://www.instagram.com/mystic_merryl/

MIRACLES THAT TRAVELED THE WORLD

Myra Swan Kotze

My life has been shaped by miracles in ways I still struggle to put into words. There are two miracles in my story — and the second would never have been possible without the first.

Just over 55 years ago, my mother was told she was about to die.

Doctors believed she had a cyst on her ovaries that was about to burst. At that time, there were no sonars, no scans — only a diagnosis and urgency. The doctor told my father to get her to a hospital immediately. If the cyst burst, she would not survive.

They were living in Christiana at the time, a small town in South Africa and my dad had to drive more than a hundred kilometers to Kimberley, praying the whole way that she would make it in time.

When the doctors opened her up, they discovered the impossible. The "cyst" had arms. And legs. And a head. It was a healthy fetus.

My mother was already three or four months pregnant at the age of 47, after giving birth to four sons — each labor lasting nearly 48 hours. Her womb was weak and the doctors warned this pregnancy was extremely risky.

She was released to go home — and to keep me alive, she had to keep moving. The moment she rested, her womb went into contractions. So she walked... day and night... around our home... relentlessly. She walked so that I could live. I am here because she refused to lie down.

That was my first miracle. And everything that came after, flowed from it.

Many years later, the miracle returned — this time through my daughter.

I have only one daughter and I love her beyond words. She is my whole world. Losing her was never something my heart could even imagine surviving.

During COVID, she became pregnant while living in Thailand. She was healthy, glowing and everything seemed perfect — until suddenly it wasn't. Her blood pressure rose dangerously high and she was diagnosed with severe preeclampsia. She had to be moved urgently from Koh Samui Island to Phuket — hours of travel by ferry and road while her body was already shutting down. By the time they arrived at the hospital, the doctors told her the truth: Her condition was extremely severe. The baby had to be born within 24 hours.

And the chances of her baby surviving were zero.

Because of COVID restrictions, her husband was taken away from her immediately. She was left completely alone with that information — for hours. No partner. No family. No comfort. She was falling apart.

The next day, my husband and I arrived in Phuket to be with her. By then, induction had already started because she wanted to try for a normal birth. The doctors came out to speak to us and told us something no mother ever wants to hear: The chances were very high that we would lose both of them.

I remember my heart breaking in a way I didn't know was possible. I didn't want to lose my daughter. I didn't want to lose the little boy we had already fallen in love with through every scan and every heartbeat.

So I prayed. I prayed for hours. I prayed with everything in me.

After hours of nothing happening, the doctors made the decision to take her into theatre. I arrived just before they did — but I was not allowed to see her. No one was. Not me and not her husband. She had been in total isolation from the moment she entered the hospital. I didn't see her again until she came out of surgery.

My grandson was born at just 28 weeks and taken straight into neonatal intensive care. He was impossibly small. His skin was still translucent. There were tubes everywhere... breathing, feeding, monitoring; more machines than I had ever seen attached to a human being.

Because of COVID, we couldn't hold him. They brought him to a window once so that we could see him. He looked like a tiny newborn monkey — fragile, raw and fighting. For 30 days, we stayed in Phuket. He had brain bleeds and infections; scans that showed progress and scans that terrified us.

But he stayed alive. I have never seen a little human fight so hard to be here.

When he finally came home, the questions started: Is his brain okay? Will he develop normally? A doctor, with no bedside manner at all, simply said, "so you're worried he might be stupid."

We didn't know. We could only wait. And then he grew.

Today, he is 4 years old. We celebrated his fourth birthday on January 11, 2026. He is intelligent, loving, magical and full of life. He is everything they said he might not be.

And his miracle didn't stop there. When he was just one year old, he traveled the world with us — from Thailand to Venezuela and then on to Mexico, where we now live permanently.

A miracle that began in South Africa....
Continued in Thailand....
And now lives and grows in Mexico.

One miracle made the next one possible.
I was nearly not here.
And he was nearly not here.

The power of prayer. The power of belief. The power of God's hand across generations — it is real.

These miracles don't feel normal to me. They feel extraordinary.

And yet, I know this to be true: Miracles are normal.

Myra Swan Kotze - Quantum Wealth & Energetic Business Mentor

https://leverageher.com/

https://www.facebook.com/MyraSwanKotzeLeverageHer/

WHEN YOUR BODY SPEAKS

Dr. Rani Thanacoody

Miracles have always fascinated me, from my childhood when I met my spiritual master Sri Satya Sai Baba, in 1982. He would manifest various objects such as lingam (cosmic egg) and vibhuti (sacred ash) for the devotees who would visit him in his ashram in India. I thought that only spiritual masters or ascended masters possessed those powers; just like Jesus would manifest miracles in several stories in the Bible. But I never thought that I could one day manifest my own miracles.

Miracles have always occurred in my life, but I never paid much attention. One miracle, however, that has left a profound mark on me occurred when I was around the age of 17. I was experiencing a lot of pain in my right knee, and it was affecting my day-to-day functioning and mobility. One day my father took me to the orthopaedic consultant. I was told that I needed immediate surgery. He advised me to also have the left knee operated on at the same time. He believed that I would suffer from pain in that other knee in the future. I was very shocked by his diagnosis. We followed his advice to have the surgery done in the coming days. I really did not want to have this surgery! I was praying and asking God from the time I left the doctor's office, to save me from having to have the surgery. At that time, there was no internet and no Google to read and find out more information about the knee pain that I was experiencing. The doctor's advice was like a court verdict.

As the day of the surgery was approaching, I felt a voice inside of me whispering that 'I should not go for the surgery'. I told my mother how I was feeling. I knew the surgery was not the right solution for me. I was so anxious and uncomfortable with that quick decision made by the doctor. Finally, the day of the surgery arrived. Early that morning, I was packing my clothes in a suitcase, as I would have to stay in the private hospital for a few days. I felt so uncomfortable. I was praying in my heart that I did not have to go through with the surgery, and I told my mother about my feelings and my prayers.

Suddenly the phone rang and when I picked it up, the receptionist from the hospital was on the other end. I could clearly hear her sharp voice echoing in my ear. She was calling to inform me that my surgery had been cancelled due to an urgent caesarean surgery needed on a patient, and that the operating theatre would be unavailable for my surgery. I was very surprised and instantly relieved, and I felt joy within me. I rushed to tell my parents. Nobody could believe that the surgery was suddenly cancelled. My parents asked me if I had definitely heard the receptionist's message clearly. I was so thankful to God for that news. It was a miracle indeed. My prayers were answered.

After a few weeks I found a shop where I could purchase some comfortable shoes, and I never experienced such knee pain again.

Another miracle I experienced in my late twenties occurred when I was searching for a new job, whilst also considering studying for a higher degree. On the day I was meant to start the new job, I got very sick and could not breathe. I was feeling stressed and I informed the manager that I could not join his company. He was so angry that he wrote about me in a local newspaper. On that same afternoon, while checking my emails, I saw that I had been offered an international scholarship for a duration of four years, with paid living expenses, by an Australian university. I was very excited and realised that declining that job was a blessing in disguise. My agent was very astonished as I was the first person in my country to benefit from this scholarship. It was a miracle.

Miracles have become a daily experience in my life since November 2024 as I delved more deeply into healing my inner child and peeling away those layers of trauma. During my daily commute on buses and trains, people unexpectedly offered me their seats or opened doors to let me in even though they had been waiting before me.

In addition, I meet like-minded people online and at local events effortlessly. I am invited to speak at webinars, international conferences and local events that lead to other speaking engagements. I often encounter strangers on the streets who engage in conversations with me. I am offered opportunities to write in peer-reviewed books and journals in my field of research.

The miracles keep multiplying day by day and I gratefully embrace them. For me now, miracles are normal as I raise my vibrations to a higher frequency.

Dr Rani Thanacoody – Clinical Hypnotherapist and Inspirational Speaker
https//marsvenuscoachrani.com
https://drranithanacoody.com

A Miracle Of One's Own

Dr. Robin Fricke

In the Book of Miracles, miracles mean life. Miracles are healing. Miracles are habits and involuntary. Miracles are natural. Miracles are everyone's right. Prayer is the medium of miracles. Through miracles, love is expressed.

I was told that miracles are perceptions because they are our thoughts. I know now what that means for me. Miracles are examples of right-thinking, aligning our perception with truth, as God created it. Miracles bear witness to truth. Miracles transcend the body. Miracles reawaken the awareness. The spirit, not the body, is in the altar of truth. Miracles represent freedom from fear. Miracles inspire gratitude. Miracles restore the mind to its fullness. Miracles honor you because you are lovable.

The Book of Miracles made me wonder whether I believe that miracles are perceptions. I started to think about what my true thoughts were about having a massive stroke, which then had me thinking about the trajectory of my life and the changes that took place without my permission.

How can a stroke take the last 15-20 years of my memories and my ability to remember, be a miracle? Or how about my little Douglas Jr., whom I lost when

I was 33 weeks pregnant. I started having mysterious chronic health issues at the age of 6. I almost died when I was 17 years old from having Strep-B, which then caused my body to go septic. Or when I was abandoned and then physically and sexually abused, lied to and betrayed. I was 15 years old, homeless, scared for my life and all alone.

How could these painful, awful things be miracles?

Well, the first miracle is that all those painful, awful things happened for me and by me, not to me. They shaped me into the beautiful, kind woman I am today. That is a miracle!

When I was just a girl in the hospital, fighting for my life, it showed me how many people cared for and loved me. I didn't feel loved or cared for before that, so this new sense of love gave me hope and I pulled through. That is a miracle.

The beautiful little baby boy I never got to hold came to me that morning in a dream (this was before I knew he had died). I had just given birth, and in my dream he was the size of a 6-8 month old baby sitting on my hip, just looking at me with his big blue eyes; a shiny, little, round, perfect, bald head, the strongest posture and the biggest smile. He was a happy baby. I remember waking up thinking I was going to have a big baby boy. That was when I found out that he had passed away while I was sleeping. He came to me, he let me hold him and he let me know that he loved me - and I knew that he knew I loved him too and that he was ok. That was a miracle.

A year later, I got pregnant with another beautiful baby boy, Mason Douglas West, who was born with olive skin and long, dark black hair, weighing 9 lbs 2 oz. I was told that I could most likely never carry a baby full term again, but here he was... Mason - my miracle baby. That is a miracle.

The chronic mysterious illnesses changed not only my perspective on Western medicine, but they also opened up my curiosity about myself spiritually, mentally and emotionally. They caused me to search for the secret to whole health, especially women's health. I became an authority on my own health and I now help women around the world rediscover theirs. That is a miracle.

The stroke gave me so much more than it took from me. That is a miracle.

I used to be angry, shameful, guilty, embarrassed and sad, carrying so much. I didn't know that these painful, nasty things were miracles leading me to exactly where I am today. I am proud of where I have been, where I am at and where I am headed.

Do me a favor and work on getting to know yourself. Figure out how to turn your pain into gratitude. Don't be ashamed of the things you think you have done or not done. You have the choice to decide who you want to be and where you want to go, so don't let your pain keep you in the past and stuck in the muck. Hold hands with your pain and pull her out of the muck!

P.S.S. YOU ARE A MIRACLE, XOXO

Robin Fricke - HHP, INHC, PhD
https://robinfricke.com
https://www.facebook.com/robin.stockdale.5

An Unlikely Miracle

Rev. Robyn Accetturo, LCSW

Miracles are powerful reminders that we are Spiritual Beings sharing our human experience. In 1987, working on my master's degree in social work, I had my first prophetic dream. It came true right before my eyes. I had another dream about the same patient who passed away a few days later, exactly like in my dream. The Universe was leading me on a Spiritual journey that continues today. I took my vows to become an Ordained Spiritualist Minister in 2008.

My husband and I were introduced to Spiritualism as a road to discovering the knowledge and the truth behind the power of my dreams. Our first mediumship readings profoundly changed our lives. Since we were both psychiatric social workers, we questioned everything about our experience. We paid a Medium to talk to our dead loved ones, yet our psychiatric patients took psychotropic medications while others had ECT to stop their hallucinations. The more I questioned God, the more my psychiatric patients answered.

One morning, I visited a bipolar patient named Billy, to do his psychosocial assessment. When asked his reason for admission he responded, "so I can meet you, Robyn." Billy gave me a 100% accurate clairvoyant reading of my life! He shared stories from my childhood through to the present moment. It felt weirdly uncanny.

Billy told me that the patients in my therapy group were getting excited about themselves again. He said the group was there to help me to give feedback on the intuitive work I was sharing in order to help members become their authentic Spiritual selves. Billy ended our session with, "I've been in this same level of functioning therapy group in this hospital for years. You are onto something big here, Robyn. I encourage you to learn about how a 4-stroke-cycle combustion engine operates, so I can help you figure out and write down your theory on feelings. Many people will be helped, especially men. Trust yourself. Trust me. Trust God. Just do it please, so I can go home."

Billy was a master auto mechanic. I bought the book *Auto Repair for Dummies* as directed and studied the 4-stroke cycle combustion engine with Billy for three weeks. Billy was adamant that I had to figure out how we as Spirit, operate our human body similarly as to how a 4-stroke-cycle combustion engine operates a car. I applied the life skills tools I was teaching in group therapy to this 4-stroke cycle combustion engine. Billy said we were creating a mental health/spiritual operations manual. He loved seeing immediate results in others who applied the knowledge when coming together in our meetings.

After my first prophetic dream, my husband and I went to a Spiritualist camp in the United States to get answers. I asked a Medium if God could pick someone else for whatever these dreams were preparing me. She laughed and said, "No, but you can ask God to slow it down. You've been chosen for this Sacred Contract." She instructed me to say a prayer to ask God to slow my experience down and to take away my fear. I did. God answered.

I dreamed of a Shaman. We shared a dance of rebirth... no words... in a grass hut with a mud floor, to the sound of a drum that felt like a universal heartbeat. Our naked bodies were covered in vernix caseosa. Underneath were white fluorescent painted ancient symbols. The Shaman wore a necklace of animal teeth, claws, seeds, crystals and more. He had a Buddha-like belly. His smile eased my fear. We danced to the rhythm of the drum, melding us as One, in a Soulful dance of Universal Light and Love. Every breath merged with the heartbeat of Mother Earth. My fear melted away with every step. Peace, grace, and mercy penetrated my entire being with a new-found freedom and openness I find hard to describe.

After three weeks of working with Billy, I was staring out of the window when my dream of the Shaman floated into my awareness. I heard Billy shift his weight and I came out of my trance. As I glanced at Billy it dawned on me, that he was the Shaman in my dream! The second our eyes met, Billy let out a chuckle. "I was wondering when you were going to figure that out, Robyn!" I felt incredibly grateful for the Universe's Divine Intervention on my behalf. Meeting and working with Billy was a Sacred Contract we had both agreed to before we incarnated.

Billy was discharged from the psychiatric unit for the last time. His son called to say that Billy had passed away peacefully in his sleep a few days later. Thank you Billy, for a job well done! I just launched my 2nd book, 'I am the Reluctant Messiah and So Are YOU'. I have much to thank Billy for...and God. Miracles are REAL.

Rev. Robyn Accetturo, LCSW – Licensed Clinical Social Worker

www.revrobyn.com

www.facebook.com/profile.php?id=61556977907852

From Burnout To Inner Light. My Journey Back To Self-Love

Roeleke Klein Ikkink

At 41, on the outside, my life looked solid; a cozy house, a 15-year-old son who is a dedicated athlete and a new luxury car on the way. On the inside, I was crumbling. I found myself in my third burnout, exhausted, disconnected from my own life and no longer the mother I wanted to be. One Friday, walking home from work with my dog, I hit rock bottom. I was tired in every sense of the word. I knew things had to change, but I had no idea how. By Monday, I had resigned from my job.

Looking back, that rock bottom moment was the Universe saying, "this is enough!"

For me, that was a miracle. I had been weighing the decision to leave for over a year, constantly crossing my own boundaries, trying to hold everything together.

Through that moment, I learned something essential: I am always protected… I am safe… I am loved. And that no matter how chaotic life may feel, there is always a greater purpose in the making. This lesson has stayed with me ever since. To this day, when I find myself in the middle of a life storm, I consciously take the time to zoom out and to observe what is really happening. I return to my core and only then do I step back in. And when I cannot do that on my own, I have deep, unshakable trust in my 'define posse', as I call them. They have my back. Always. Even when I am mad at them.

Let's go back to the moment I resigned from my job.

After that, my journey inward began.

Early in this process, I was told something that gave words to an experience I had carried my entire life. I was told that I am someone with a strong intuitive sensitivity; someone who naturally perceives the world beyond the visible layers. I perceive multiple layers of reality at the same time and I can sense and move between different worlds and dimensions. Most people experience life through one dimension and experience the world very differently.

This explained why, as a child, I often felt different, misunderstood and out of sync with others. I did not understand why people did what they did.

I also learned that I carry a deep responsibility, not only for myself but also for the collective energy we are all part of. I was here with a purpose and it was time to step into that truth.

As my inner exploration deepened, I confronted buried fears, anger, grief and pain. I learned to feel rather than to be numb and to face trauma after trauma, from this life, previous lives and echoes of lives carried through generations on both my mother and father's sides.

Healing often focuses on the maternal line, but my journey asked me to look at both. Being of mixed Surinamese and Dutch heritage, for example, the legacy of slavery lives in my DNA from both sides. I carry the pain of the oppressed as well as the imprints of the system itself. A truth that requires deep honesty, compassion and responsibility.

Some wounds took hours to heal, some took days and some took years. With each cycle of feeling, healing and release, I grew stronger, clearer and more rooted in my own heart.

I realized I had spent decades rationalizing everyone's behavior. Understanding why people act the way they do, seeing their pain, reading their hidden wounds, until I forgot how much it affected me. I could intellectualize everything around me, yet I had no idea how deeply I had absorbed it all.

I also recognized a pattern. I had unconsciously chosen relationships that diminished me, or people who found my love too much and did not know how to cherish it. I decided not to pursue romantic relationships anymore, until I understood why I attracted these dynamics and why I allowed mistreatment.

My greatest lesson came in realizing that unconditional self-love is the foundation upon which everything else stands. Authenticity, growth, self-worth, respect, abundance, joy and so on... they all rest on it. Everything in our lives can be traced back to the way we love ourselves. Why do we attract painful relationships? Why do we allow others to treat us poorly? Why is our loyalty to others greater than our loyalty to ourselves?

I discovered that every choice, at its core, is a choice between fear or love. The more love I cultivated for myself, the more I naturally chose from love. That choice radiated outward and brought healing to the people around me as well.

Now, at 49, I have taken another big leap. I moved from the Netherlands to Curaçao, a beautiful island in the Caribbean, about 9,000 kilometers away. The reason I went there goes back to a meditation I did about eight years ago. In it, I was told that Curaçao would be my home. I had never been there, so I thought, "well, we'll see." That feeling kept returning and so in 2019, I went to Curaçao for the first time. I hadn't flown in 16 years and was struggling with a fear of flying.

Yet during the flight, I had the unmistakable feeling that I was flying home, not just on vacation. The moment I stepped off the plane, every fiber in my body knew that this was my home. Six years later, in 2025, I finally took the leap and with a smaller bank account than I expected, but carrying within me a heart full of love and trust, I made the move.

To date, I have completed two poetry books and I am honored to be one of the authors in this book, 'Miracles Are Normal', and I am currently working on multiple books: three for adults and one for children. Healing, surrendering to the light, and consciously choosing love is no longer something I do. It has become who I am.

I often think back to that Friday walk with my dog. The exhaustion and despair that once felt unbearable now feels like the opening chapters of my greatest adventure. If my journey helps even one soul remember their own capacity for transformation, then every step was worth it.

Miracles, I now understand, are not distant or rare. They are woven into the fabric of everyday courage, the courage to choose love over fear, to feel and to rise again and again.

And that love... that real, pure, soul-felt love, is the greatest miracle of all.

Roeleke Klein Ikkink – Embodied Self Love Guide

https://withloveacademy.com/

https://www.instagram.com/withloveacademy

After The Storm

Rosey McBride

It was a rainy and windy night. I could hear the raindrops falling on the windowsill... the trees rustling in the wind. The weather was a precise interpretation of how my life was going.

I should have been celebrating my big win - one of my biggest accomplishments was getting out of debt and acquiring financial security for my son and I. Instead, I was sitting on the floor of my room, throwing myself a pity party (something I caught myself doing often).

My life had turned upside down. From the stress of my chauvinistic boss, my ex-husband fighting me in court for full custody of our son, to the recent loss of my mother who had lost her battle with cancer, I felt alone with no one to share my victories or the best part of my day, or better yet, my sorrows and fears.

To make matters worse, two close friends had relocated for financial reasons.

I understood that life was hard, not just for me but for many people around me. I felt I was always taking one step forward and two steps back. I would sit and wonder how I got here. How did I go down the rabbit hole? How was I always treading water, trying not to drown? Anger would fill me as I acknowledged the root of my problem. Me! I was the problem.

I had become weak and had allowed my partner at the time to break down my self-esteem… from calling my religion a cult that I had practiced my whole life, to not wanting me to see my friends or family.

My life did a 180° turn when I came home from work one day. He had ended the lease at the apartment where we lived and tried to tell me that things would be better when we moved, and that if I refused, he would take our son away from me. So, here I sat, angry at myself that I wasn't stronger.

The next morning, after the storm when the sun came out, I was feeling a little better. I always felt better after the rain because the sound and smell of the rain have a calming effect on the mind, reducing stress and promoting relaxation. I recognized that after every storm, there was a rainbow. But I continued throwing myself a pity party for months to come. I had to snap out of this. I had to learn how to dance in the rain. I had so much to be grateful for. My turning point came totally unexpectedly:

One evening, after a long, dreadful day at work, I checked the mail and as I was sifting through it, a postcard from the local fellowship read, "Are you anxious?" It seemed to me a miracle presented itself in the form of a postcard. It came at the right time in my life when I least expected it. This postcard had my name written all over it. They were advertising a women's study group. This event was a blessing in disguise. The next thing I knew, I had registered and started attending the meetings.

We always started with prayers. All the ladies asked for prayers for health, job security, or finding a partner. I found myself asking for prayers for peace in my heart. It felt good to know that I wasn't alone. Due to this experience, I started coming out of my shell… I started becoming that young, vibrant lady that people close to me viewed me as always having been.

My new journey led me to attend social gatherings and join professional networking groups. During my downtime, I also filled my free time listening to and watching motivational videos on Youtube. This led to me to watch The Law of Attraction and learning about affirmations. I began practicing what I learned. I started working through my insecurities and my self-esteem. I engaged in doing more things that I love. Life is short.

Now, I work as a teacher and a certified life coach, but this journey wasn't just about a career change — it was about rediscovering myself.

One day, a young woman approached me after a workshop I had led. Tears glistened in her eyes as she said, "You've helped me believe that I can start over." Her words brought me back to that stormy night when I thought I had lost everything and yet here I was, standing tall and helping others find their way.

I realized that my past wasn't a weight anymore, it was my fuel. Every setback had been a stepping stone and every storm, a lesson in resilience. As I drove home that evening, the sunset painted the sky in brilliant hues of orange and pink, and I couldn't help but smile. Life would always have its storms, but now I knew that after the rain, the sun always shines - and I would always shine with it.

Rosey McBride – Teacher, Life Coach
www.makemyliferosey.com
https://www.instagram.com/roseym.lifecoach/

The Miracle In Surrender

Sherri Favors

What was I thinking? Why did I agree to write this chapter? These were my first thoughts after I said yes. Then it began, the negative self-talk. Why would anyone want to hear my story? Were they really miracles? Can I even do this? I'm not a writer. I don't even have time. How am I supposed to fit this in with everything else? I can't do it. A monsoon of thoughts flooded my mind.

Anxiety filled my body, followed by disappointment. Here I was, believing I had done the inner work, that I had overcome my limiting beliefs, that I had a Can-Do attitude. I dedicated years to releasing negative belief patterns and reprogramming my mindset. But when faced with a task that took me out of my comfort zone, I fell apart.

So, I sat, I became very still, and I tried to figure out what was causing all of this resistance. Deep down, I knew that I was capable. It wasn't that I didn't have a story to tell; miracles have always been a part of my life. In fact, they were so common that they didn't seem like miracles. Then the answer materialized: control. While my life wasn't perfect, I understood it; I found comfort in the predictable. Losing control, even a little, terrified me. I wasn't always this way.

As a child, surrender was a natural part of my life and it opened the door to miracles. One example of this is the grocery miracle, which showed me the power of surrender in creating miracles.

On the Monday before Valentine's Day in my 6th-grade year, my teacher handed out the sign-up sheet for the Valentine's Day party. A feeling of dread overcame me as I stared at the list, trying to figure out what on earth I could bring that my mom could afford. You see, my parents divorced when I was younger and although my mother was very hard-working, money was tight. Making sure I was safe, warm, clothed and fed was the priority; purchasing party food was not. So, while I heard my peers excitedly discussing the hot wings, cupcakes and sub sandwiches they were contributing, I meekly wrote the word "chips".

When I got home, I told my mom about the party and she took me to Fred's, the local grocery store. She gave me $3.30 and a list with seven items: chips, bread, hot sauce, mayonnaise, ketchup, mustard, and sweet relish. She told me, "Get the chips and the bread. See if any of the other things are on sale and get that."

So I walked toward the entrance of Fred's and stopped at the sliding doors. I lifted my $3.30 and my shopping list to the sky and quietly prayed, "God, this is what I have and this is what I need. You said You're my provider." I took a deep breath, surrendered and walked inside. I put the chips in my shopping basket. They were $0.99. I saw the hot sauce and the sweet relish next. They were both on sale for $0.75 each. My total had reached $2.49, and I still hadn't gotten the bread. I went to the bread aisle. Right above the bread, the sign read '$1.25'. I didn't have enough. At that point, I began thinking about what I could put back. But before I decided, I picked up a loaf of bread and put it in my basket.

Underneath the loaf was a $5.00 bill. I said a quick "thank you" and collected the rest of the items and purchased them. When I arrived in our car with all the items on the list, a receipt and change, my mother was surprised. Interestingly, she didn't ask any questions. She did, however, send me a few more times with long shopping lists and very little money. Every single time, I was able to purchase each item and bring back change. The miracle didn't happen the same way each time. Sometimes I found money, sometimes people would pay for it. Once, the cashier paid for it. I never asked anyone for help; I just surrendered, and everything fell into place.

In all honesty, surrendering is scary. It was scary in 6th grade and it is still scary now. Yet, it is essential for growth. Without surrender, there is no risk. Without surrender, there is no progress. Back then, I had no choice. Now I have options. I am choosing to surrender, not because I should, but because it creates the stream through which miracles flow, and I believe it can do the same for you.

Sherri Favors - Emotional Energy Coach
https://tinyurl.com/favored81
https://www.instagram.com/favored81/

Beginning Again – Lessons From Training Camp

Dr. Solveig Berg

Since 2020, I have been offering training in morphic field reading – Conscious Reading. It was a suc-cess from the start. Clients came by themselves and recommended me further. My business peaked in 2022 with record sales and a hunger for more. Miracles were normal in my everyday life, and I told the Universe that I was ready for the next level – to have even more clients, more money, more reputation.

But instead of progress, the year 2023 brought a downfall. I met a new partner and soon found myself in a toxic and abusive relationship, too dependent to leave. This relationship robbed me of my balance, my calm, my energy and all my money. And it took me until February 2024 to free myself. This is also when I received the last strike from him: not taking over the flat lease as promised but making me move out and then moving out himself – leaving me with the cost of three months' rent.

It was the lowest moment of my life and I had no positive perspective; the echo of my steps and my voice bouncing off the empty walls like the perfect reflection of my current situation. But within me I suddenly knew: the Universe was not neglecting my wish for a next level – it had sent me a training camp instead, to properly prepare myself for that next level!!

This is when things shifted and miracles became normal.

The first miracle I realized was that the couch I wanted to sell had been left behind... so I could sleep, work and eat on it. The moving company had forgotten my blanket, my pillow AND... the yoga mat. The next day, one of my colleagues, a Yin Yoga teacher, invited me to her yoga lessons for free.

I went to the secondhand shop and bought a plate, a fork, a knife, a spoon, a glass and a small pot in which to warm food. Nothing distracted me anymore and I could focus solely on what I needed to do next.

I applied for a job in ambulant care as they offered opportunities for untrained people and always needed substitutes. On the way to my first working day, I sat in my car and made the decision that I wouldn't pity myself now and lament on how deep I had sunk, instead, I would create for myself the best experience ever.

It was a fantastic experience. Taking care of and helping old people has proven to be a very satisfying and nourishing job. I surprised myself at how good I actually was at handling the various situations and after work, I came home with a new sense of fulfillment. My spiritual business had always ful-filled me, but it also had become a hunt for the next adrenaline high in the form of higher amounts of clients and income. There was always the feeling of not good enough, not high enough.

Meeting old and sick people did not drag me down – it made me so grateful for my health instead. It made me grateful to just wake up in the morning, being able to breathe, being able to go to the toilet and take a shower by myself.

The next miracle was that I was offered a little job as a piano player at my children's school (one of my childhood dreams). My piano was "parked" in the barn of a friend, and I remember summer afternoons sitting in the shady barn, practicing. It took my mind off all my worries and made my body re-lax into the music. And... I learned something very important : slowing down.

To be proficient in new piano pieces in a short time, it is necessary to start playing the pieces painfully and achingly slowly. But I could literally observe how my playing gained momentum, space and speed. I then decided that this would be how I would build up my business again. Slowly and steadily.

I searched my soul for several months on how I wanted my business to be, how I wanted to feel with it, and suddenly the idea of a newsletter with a daily energy forecast came up. I put myself into this project 100% and the resonance was amazing. I gained new clients, bookings came in again and many people told me, "I am canceling a lot of email lists these days, but I will always keep yours".

Soon after, I was ready to take the big leap of trust. I transformed my 5-week online training program into an academy with a year-long schedule. As I wanted to move slowly, I gave myself three months in which to advertise and prepare the academy. As of today, the (German-speaking) academy totals in excess of 50 students already.

My message has always been: Everybody is clairvoyant. And my mission is to prove it.

Dr. Solveig Berg - Field Reading Expert and Author

https://consciousreading.com

https://consciousreading.com/newsletter

Where The Heart Leads

Souli Yates

I have come to understand that miracles are a part of life. Life itself is a miracle. However, there are those moments that take your breath away. This is a story of a day of such moments.

Many years ago, at the beginning of my awakening and my personal healing, while attending a course named 'Awakening your Light Body', there was a buzz in the air. Someone on the course announced that she had tickets for a 4-day teaching experience with The Dalai Lama in London.

It was as if a lightning bolt hit my friend and I. Almost as one we said that we would go. Everyone on the course said that we would never get tickets if we didn't already have them. They had sold out straight away; it would be impossible.

This is the magical part... without a word of doubt we both knew that we were already there. In this space of unspoken certainty, we booked the hotel and the train to and from the venue.

We arrived on the morning of the first day of the training still with no idea of the 'how-to's' but with a knowing that it was a given. We went to what appeared to be the entrance to see if we could get some return tickets from the box office. As we were waiting, a bus full of monks made their way into the venue. One monk stopped and looked at us - there was an energetic exchange almost as if there was some kind of unspoken telepathic message, a transmission.

As that moment passed there was a gust of wind and the leaves all about us took flight, ushering us to move to the other side of the venue. We ended up where everybody else was waiting for the doors to open. Standing on the steps, there was a feeling of something huge about to happen, a reverence.

While waiting, a chance meeting with my first contemporary dance teacher guided us to exactly where we needed to be for the biggest miracle of a day full of synchronicity and serendipity.

We sat down and overheard a conversation in front of us. A group of ladies were saying how sad it was that they were unable to make it and they were discussing what to do with their tickets. We were their solution, their miracle and so we ended up with two sets of tickets for all 4 days!

This whole experience was pivotal for me. We learned so much and received more than we could ever have imagined.

We didn't take notes; we sat and absorbed the phenomenal transmissions. The words were golden of course, but there was a deeper wisdom carried energetically. I am profoundly grateful for this amazing experience and for the miracles that flowed our way from a space of knowing.

I loved the way that The Dalai Lama was also teaching something that another great teacher tried to share many moons ago; that we are all capable of doing miraculous things, that we are the same; there is no need to place anyone on a pedestal. We create miracles every moment, with every breath, with every thought, with every word. What we chose is the spice, the magical ingredient. The message? Choose only love, love is the answer to every question.

There was a beautiful moment when another miracle occurred on one of the nights. A fire alarm took us all out into the car park outside the Hotel. I turned to see who was beside me. It was The Dalai Lama in his dressing gown. I was too shy to talk to him but his smile and warmth said it all. We stood side-by-side until it was all clear and we returned to our rooms. Such a treasured memory.

The key to the Miracles of this story was the 'Knowing'. Treasure those times when your heart shows you the way and follow it. Your heart will never steer you in the wrong direction. Simply allow for miracles to flow into your life. How? By noticing the little moments, the small miracles, the everyday miracles that can pass us by if we don't look; the smile from a stranger that lifts you up... the beauty of nature... Life itself is a miracle. There is so much to notice when you pay attention to the 'Now'. With presence, miracles gain momentum and will find that you will flow with serendipity and synchronicity, and thus miracles become your truth. Life becomes Magical. It takes practice, but it is so worth it. You are worth it. Don't waste another moment, gather the little gems of existence.

Souli Yates - Advanced Channel, Spiritual Mentor
https://souli-yates-portal.my.canva.site/souli-yates-portal
https://www.facebook.com/souli.yates

Miracles: The Highest Form Of Love

Stephaanie Hartwell

I fully trust that I am the Universe and that I am creating my most magnificent life!

Years ago, before any type of awakening or consciousness, miracles were something fantastical; they were outside of myself... miraculous, infrequent, random and contingent upon my obedience or worthiness. They were so out of the ordinary and filled with mystery that I didn't feel worthy of them. Miracles were something from God and only God, blessed upon me only if I was righteous and obedient to the rules and laws that my religion set forth.

Even the dictionary defines them as an act of God, something miraculous... an amazing event... the extraordinary... something that happens that is not an ordinary occurrence in our lives!

This religious dogma was how I was taught and what I believed through religion and society and is also what kept me from experiencing miracles very often.

I discovered that through trauma, our heart remembers. It remembers the little simple hurts, the big horrific acts of abuse and the emotions we couldn't express or feel in those moments. They accumulate and shut down our heart so that we are unable to receive love or miracles.

In the early stages of my Awakening, my oldest daughter experienced a home invasion. Breaking the basement window, the intruders worked their way through the house to the upstairs bedroom where she was. She climbed into a closet to hide and called 911 to direct the police to her immediately.

As the police arrived and the intruders realized they were caught, one of them jumped into the closet right next to my daughter; they were touching shoulders.

She was breathing heavily, still whispering to 911 telling them the intruder was standing next to her in the closet. All the time the intruder had no idea she was there.

How can that be? A miracle?

When the police stormed into the room, my daughter jumped out of the closet, letting them know he was still in there. They apprehended him and the others as well.

While telling me of her experience, I visualized angels' wings around her. She had been fully protected! At this time in her life, she was in her alignment to her divine truth and purpose. Her frequency was in full alignment with the Miracle of protection, which is what began my perspective shift on what a miracle truly was.

It changed from being a 'once-in-a-while' act of God (one I needed to be worthy of), to an everyday occurrence in my life.

This perspective evolved as I started to practice loving, forgiving and healing. I focused on what was going 'right' in my life rather than my traumatic past and what was currently going 'wrong.' Doing this, created profound changes within me and with those around me.

This focus created evidence which accumulated daily, reminding every cell in my body of my divine birthright: I am love. Only when I learned to receive that love and light back into my heart, did I recognize miracles as everyday occurrences, confirming that I was worthy of love.

My frequency elevated immensely by embodying love more than I ever had before. Consequently, miracles became a part of who I was as a Spiritual Divine Being, an everyday act of love... beautiful, divine, magnetic changes on the timeline.

"In order to receive a miracle, you must be in vibrational alignment with it." Lee Harris November Energy update 2025

Over the last 25 years, I realized it wasn't someone or something outside myself, blessing me because I was being good or obedient; it was a gradual vibrational shift happening within me. Thus, my light reflected into the world and the world reflected that light back to me in the form of miracles. They weren't fantastical or unbelievable anymore; they were silent actions that move through our lives within the deepest parts of our heart, sometimes unknown and undetected, quietly acknowledged and transforming.

Life becomes a series of miracles when I am in alignment with my truest Divine light, my magnificence and my birthright. Miracles are the inspiration of our souls, the expression of our highest vision of joy.

This life in alignment has been nothing short of enchanting.

Mysterious sums of money that show up in my bank account; a friend calling at my lowest point offering a beautiful gift of love, soothing my aching heart; the volunteer piano gig at the hospital I had longed to initiate, simply falling perfectly into place and reviving the joy I had lost. And, most recently, after making a plea to the Divine for help paying my bills, I was gifted a $100 tip from a beautiful couple. Feeling so moved, I began to cry, releasing emotions of gratitude. As I looked up from the steering wheel, there in front of me stood a tree in the shape of a heart - the symbol of love I needed in that exact moment, acknowledging that I was fully supported because I asked to be.

Today, I know I don't have to rely on something outside of myself to determine my worth. I am innately worthy to receive these miracles of love every day and be seen as important in this world. It is my divine birthright to vibrate at the frequency of love and understand that we are literally the miracle - the sacred representation of who we are!

Stephaanie Hartwell - Alchemist, Energy & Sound Specialist, Spiritual Mentor, Reiki Master Teacher
https://www.lightalchemy.biz/
https://www.facebook.com/StephaanieHart

Divine Paths To Parenthood: A Life Of Love, Adoption, And Purpose

Steven Liss

My life has been so very blessed with what has magically always seemed like divine inspirations. Three in particular are foremost with the birth of my 2 daughters and my son, whom we adopted from three extraordinary birth-mothers who were not able to be everyday mothers to the three gifts of life that they provided to my wife and I.

My wife had a hysterectomy when she was much younger, way before our marriage, so when we got married and fell hopelessly in forever-after love, we knew that we wanted our expressions of life together to include children. We thus explored adoption options - something very foreign to us both.

We sought out guidance from a few adoption attorneys who educated us in adoption processes in California where we live. I had a family law practice that focused on child custody matters so the best interests of children was always paramount to me. My wife had been a preschool teacher and so our interest in children was symbiotic.

This process of adoption was exciting but very alien to me. I was, however, very blessed by having the parents I had. My father had Multiple Sclerosis for 46 years but lived life geared towards excellence at all times to provide maximum greatness for his 3 children, of which I was the eldest. His 'can-do-no-matter-what' approach provided me with the attitude that carried me through law school and he showed me, by example, that there was nothing I could not accomplish in this life.

This approach was multiplied exponentially by my high school wrestling coach, who drilled into us to develop the mental toughness needed to become wrestling champions and taught us to believe that there was nothing in life that we could not do, as long as we set our minds to it.

My wife and I decided to run advertisements in newspapers for pregnant women who were unable to parent their unborn children for various reasons and who wanted to 'give up' their children for adoption. I always had an empowerment philosophy in life from watching my dad and from dealing with domestic violence issues in my law practice, where I educated these women to create 'adoption plans' where they could pick their 'dream-come-true' adoptive parents to parent and love their children in ways they only dreamt of using 'open adoptions' so that their children didn't disappear into dark holes, never to be heard from again, like the closed adoptions of yesteryear.

My wife thus embarked upon this process thirty years ago, which brought us our eldest miracle of life, in our eldest daughter Paige, who we have been blessed with by seeing her graduate college and become an archeologist, seemingly so perfect in her love of digging and exploration, similar to how her birth creation was for us, when her birth mother had contacted me through my family law practice.

Almost magically, our second daughter came into our lives 9 months later, when her birth mother honored us by asking my wife and I to adopt her daughter and she has ultimately proceeded to work in the medical field.

Our son Joey was sought out by us a few years later, now wanting a boy, already having our daughters, and he is now heading into the legal field.

All of my life experiences had culminated in my law practice, which had expanded to include adoption and to working with hundreds of pregnant women empowered with adoption plans to create my life coaching program. My focus has been on empowering people to become their best, maximum selves expeditiously, due to their advanced ages; looking at their family of origin; learning from misjudgments made by their moms and dads; to not be repeated but to become their best, maximum selves as I believe everyone is entitled to be.

I have always felt so very blessed to be granted this gift to help orchestrate joint manifestations of my clients and myself, to make this complicated world a much better place – and this continues to this day.

Steven Liss - Family Formation Life Coach
Maxsuccesses.org
Steven@MaxSuccesses.org

Capability Restored

Stevie Cashion

If your biggest hurdle in life was miraculously eliminated, what could you accomplish? My name is Stevie and at the age of 51, I was given the rare privilege of answering this question.

After fighting multiple chronic pain conditions most of my adult life, I was known in my family as 'the strong one'. Every few years I was getting a shiny new diagnosis: endometriosis, migraine headaches, Loin Pain Hematuria Syndrome, recurring kidney stones, trigeminal neuralgia, fibromyalgia, recurring Shingles... With every new diagnosis, I tried conventional medicine and almost every time it failed to bring me relief. I had to find solutions on my own.

I tried everything. I drank the nasty glasses of celery juice, mixed strange powders into smoothies and tried every new supplement I heard of. I gave up red meat, sugar, dairy, cigarettes, caffeine, gluten and basically everything that gives a person joy in life. I exercised, walked laps around the yard and sat out in my shed on hot Florida summer days to induce sweating. I learned yoga, chants and affirmations. Some of these actually helped a great deal.

I had a kind of determination that could overcome anything. Or so it seemed. How can the same person who can force herself to drink a full glass of celery juice, not be able to face the dishes in her sink for days? Seriously, have you ever drunk celery juice? It is so gross. Doing the dishes should be a breeze in comparison. Instead, simple day to day tasks seemed impossible for no obvious reason. The willpower that I drew upon to sit in a sweltering hot shed with sweat dripping off of me, was replaced with anxiety and confusion. What I was experiencing is called 'Executive Dysfunction'.

As my search for relief from my chronic conditions continued, I learned that my issues were rooted in an over reactive nervous system. Every doctor, book and social media expert will tell you that reducing your stress is paramount, but none of them provided advice that helped me to achieve this. I meditated, repeated affirmations, took walks in nature, took up crafts and swallowed pills that promised to help. None of those things helped me reduce my stress - and my nervous system was more triggered than ever.

Then I discovered the HeartMath Institute in early 2025. They have developed incredibly simple, scientifically based techniques that are designed to be done on the go, to bring your body, mind and emotions into coherence. Finally, I had the answer to calming my nervous system! I used the techniques regularly. My nervous system was finally calming down for the first time in decades.

Now you might be thinking that finding HeartMath was my miracle, and while it was certainly a turning point in my healing journey, there was still something holding me back. My pain was lowering and my anxiety was melting away. The executive dysfunction, however, was still hanging in there. I was gaining a healthier body and mind, but I was still unable to face scooping the litter boxes.

It is difficult to explain executive dysfunction to someone who has never experienced it but let me try: Imagine having your hands tied together. Sure, you could still do the laundry with your hands tied, but you would have to devise a strategy. It wouldn't come naturally. It would frustrate you and you would get overwhelmed by the whole process. Eventually just the thought of trying to do the laundry would send you into a panic. It created a level of fear, resentment and guilt surrounding my inability to just get things done. Despite everything that I had overcome, I still viewed myself as incapable because of these struggles.

Then one day I heard a voice in my head say, "you can do anything". I chuckled to myself as the phrase reminded me of a pep talk and I said to myself, "Sure, I can do anything," and I put my fist up in the air and gave it a little shake, accentuating the pep talk vibe. "No" the voice corrected me, "you can do anything you need or want to do." Suddenly I realized this voice wasn't merely my inner dialogue. I felt the gravity of the statement, and it stopped me in my tracks. I stood there as this sense of knowing washed over me. I knew, from that point forward, that my executive dysfunction had been lifted.

I am now confident that I can do anything I need or want to do - and with ease. No struggling. No strategizing. No overwhelm. No gearing myself up to face the task. My capability really had been restored.

The entire world has been handed to me, and I'm not taking it for granted. Whether it is the joy of just getting up and taking a shower without giving it a second thought, or the thrill of driving for the first time in years, I am grateful. After not being employed for a decade, I decided to start my own coaching business 'Honest Wellness Coaching' LLC. I want to support other people so that they too can become 'the strong one' who finds their way to a healthy body, mind and spirit. And of course, HeartMath will be part of my offerings as I'm now a licensed HeartMath coach.

Stevie Cashion - HeartMath Coach

https://www.instagram.com/honest.wellness.coaching

honestwellnesscoaching@yahoo.com

The Solstice Shift: Reclaiming The Miracle Of Being

Tamara Benson

"Seeing a miracle will inspire you, but knowing you are a miracle will change you."— Deborah Brodie

Most think a miracle must be a lottery win or sudden healing. My greatest miracle arrived as a total physical collapse. On December 21, 2025, the winter solstice, toxic overload from my work environment brought me to my knees, stripping away the frenzy of my old world and leaving me vulnerable. This collapse allowed me to finally hear what my body had been screaming for decades. It was the divine intervention I needed to stop fighting my existence and to start choosing my life.

For years, I was a powerhouse in the restaurant industry, caught in constant motion. I was unaware that my workspace had become a toxic battlefield. Following the devastation of Hurricanes Helene and Milton, a toxic overload of mold in my workplace dismantled my health. My lungs, brain and nervous system were under siege by mycotoxins while I simply tried to do my job. Leaving that environment wasn't just a career change; it was a life-saving miracle.

I have spent sixty-three years on this earth, surviving traumatic events beginning in the womb. As a 'sensitive and gifted' soul, I often felt misaligned with the world. Looking back, the fact that I am still standing and breathing is the primary miracle. Everything leading up to that Solstice collapse was a series of quiet miracles keeping me here for this awakening.

In that silence, I realized survival depended on a radical new relationship with my vessel. I began talking to my body, listening to its needs, and thanking it for its resilience. By first honoring the miracle that I am, I became a powerful magnet for the external miracles that now flow into my life daily.

My recovery was a physical reconstruction anchored by tools that spoke the language of my body. I moved into a 99.9% pure foundation by stopping the guesses and starting the precision. Through my coach, LoriLyme Brown and advanced data from Vibrant Wellness, I saw the truth beneath the surface. I anchored my restoration through the LNB Protocols I created. On a soul level, this stands for Learn, Nourish and Believe; on a physical level, it is powered by LactiGo, Nourish and BEMER. Utilizing the BEMER for microcirculation and LactiGo for muscle recovery became the non-negotiables of my new design.

This transition peaked during a retreat with Dianne Allen, where I leaned into my 'sensitive and gifted' design. Through Safe and Sound Protocol (SSP) work and meditation, my nervous system readied itself to receive. This cleared the way for a profound breakthrough during Rosie Warburton's sound bath. In that high-frequency space, the neck and toe pain I had carried for years vanished. Inspired, I invested in angelic tuning forks to bring these vibrational modalities directly into my own healing work.

Restoration required a physical clearing of the old. I realized my external environment had to match my internal purification. I spent hours sifting through the muck of my past; tossing old restaurant paperwork, donating clothes carrying the frequency of the 'scurry' and letting go of anything that didn't vibrate at my new level of International Status. This Sovereign act of reclamation felt like a weight being lifted from my soul.

My sleep and daily rituals became a sacred ceremony of recovery. I invested in my sanctuary with RENPHO smart technology to track bio-data and a whole-home water filtration system to ensure that every drop is pure. This extended to a new washer and dryer to maintain a toxin-free cycle for the fabrics I wear. I even invested in a Purple Bed to ensure my 63-year-old body had the support it deserved. By prioritizing BEMER Sleep Mode as my primary healing tool and anchoring my environment in these high-vibe investments, I learned that a sanctuary must be 100% 'Free and Clear'. Miracles are maintained through the daily discipline of self-honor.

My plan became clear: I am no longer a woman surviving a toxic workplace, I am a curator of high-vibe healing. I started asking better questions and receiving better answers. By clearing the clutter and anchoring my health, I opened the floodgates for the ultimate miracle — the return of my Joy. This deep, serene bubbling in my spirit is the final proof that the 'ick' of the last 63 years has been purified.

The greatest part of this miracle is that Joy has finally come back to stay. Today, I am dancing; I have honored my Angels, allowing their divine frequency to guide the high-vibe healing work I now perform for others. By blending Reiki, card readings and angelic tuning forks with my own restoration wisdom, I facilitate shifts for those ready to reclaim their light. My journey has been deeply confirmed by the life-changing insights of world-renowned artist Michael Godard, reminding me that our darkest collapses are the catalysts for our highest awakening. This was harmonized during my recent retreat, where my song became 'Jesus Loves Me' — a profound anchor for my lifelong faith. Inspired by the bold, faithful testimony of global musician Jelly Roll, on the Grammy stage, I have embraced my own vision for the stage, standing anchored in the truth that the Universe created me as a miracle. Grounded by my Reiki Master certification through Kai Grace, I launched my website as a sanctuary for sensitive and gifted souls seeking sovereignty. I learned that when you are open to receiving, you realize that the Universe isn't just performing miracles around you... it created you as one.

Tamara Benson – Integrative Wellness Coach
www.TamaraBenson.com
https://www.facebook.com/tamara.benson.79

The Miracle Is You

Tara Hynes

May you always be inspired
by miraculous waves of creativity;
May you rise with the frequency of love

May you walk with comfort
nestled in your back pocket
So that the next stranger you meet
shares your delight

May you see starlight
through soul eyes
May you hear birdsong as melodic tones
permeate earth in joy with
notes of gemmed stone.

May the scent of your favourite
flowers infuse the spaces as you rest;
May sunshine keep your heart
alive with warmth as
moonbeams etch upon your skin at night

May every dawn signal rebirth
in the everlasting miracle that is
You.

This story has waited until the very last moment before print because I listened with the cosmos, looked to the sky, heard from the garden of earth, absorbed water from the rains and felt air circulate with all that is now. These are the everyday miracle moments that help support my steps towards daily presence. As I thought about you, dear reader, I imagined this book in your hands and as you opened the page, your true miraculous spirit pops.

I consulted the oracle cards as is my daily practice and the theme is clear; three words: Healing... Love... Higher Connection

Gratitude fills my heart for another reminder that as we walk life together amidst uncertainty or challenge, love ultimately leads us home. Many times when I have tumbled with fear and acted accordingly, it has taught me to realise how far away from love that I am.

Awareness kicks in and I connect with Divine Love - The Ultimate Reset. My first miracle occurred on a walk home from school on a sunny afternoon. I am wearing a full-length space-grey puffer coat - they were all in fashion in the eighties. My yellow school bag is packed with heavy textbooks. I'm ten, I'm hot and I'm thirsty. I have about another mile to walk and I start imagining a cold orange ice pop and I can even feel it on my dry tongue. But I have no money with which to buy it.

I look up at the sky and talk to God. "Please, please... I would love an ice pop", I say as I struggle to lift the school bag back onto my now indented shoulder. I open the closed buttons on this coat and wonder why I wore this thing today. I look down at the kerb and there it is... a shiny, sparkling five pence piece. "Yes", I shout as I run to the nearest shop. I may not have enough for an ice pop but this will buy an orange 'Mr Freeze' (Flavoured Frozen Ice).

My teeth can't tear open the plastic fast enough. The orange-flavoured ice sinks as it dissolves into bliss on my hot tongue. It is the best feeling and I thank God for this miracle. I still remember how good it tasted, how excited I felt and ultimately how I was heard by a Divine presence.

Today, I hold that connection to both miracles and Source. I have learnt many lessons; the truest one is that Love defines the magic, your heart creates the channel and your love connects you with Divine love.

Miracles are real.
The miracle is you.

Tara Hynes - Podcast Host of Angels Connect
https://TaraHynes.ie
https://open.spotify.com/show/5cvoypmPd1JxCRJuCseXG4

Yes, I believe in Miracles

Tena Jolley

After my annual mammogram, the clinic called and asked me to come back for a diagnostic ultrasound. Something had shown up on the screening images that needed a closer look. I told my husband that it was probably nothing, routine stuff, right? But I could tell he was already worried. His mom fought metastatic breast cancer for years before it took her; so for him, any mention of a breast issue brought everything rushing back.

At the ultrasound appointment, the radiologist explained that they wanted to get a better view of the area they had seen on the mammogram. He moved the wand over my right breast, paused a few times to take pictures, then said it looked like a solid mass with blood vessels running through it, a vascular tumor. He recommended a biopsy to find out if it was benign or something more serious. He added that most of these turn out to be benign, which helped a little, but I still saw the color leave my husband's face. We left with a follow-up biopsy scheduled and a lot of quiet in the car on the way home.

I have always leaned on my faith. I believe that God has a plan for each of us, even when life throws curveballs that make us question it. This felt like one of those moments. There's no breast cancer in my family history, so part of me kept thinking, "It'll be fine, just something they can take out and be done with."

Instead of letting worry take over, I decided I wouldn't start panicking until I had a real reason to. That became my little mantra: don't worry until it's time to worry.

But sitting still wasn't my style either. I believe in prayer, so I asked my family, my church friends and a few close people in our community to pray with me and for me; for healing, for peace, for the mass to be benign. It meant a lot knowing that they were holding me up in their own quiet ways. Every morning I would pray the same simple thing: "Please let this be nothing serious."

I also started reading up on it. I like understanding what I'm dealing with; it helps me feel less helpless. The numbers I found were encouraging. About 80% of breast lumps like this one are benign. At 30 years old, breast cancer is uncommon for someone my age. Yes, when it does happen in younger women, it can be more aggressive, but the odds still look good. Knowing that helped me stay steady. I told myself that I had every reason to be hopeful.

The biopsy was to be done in Oklahoma City, about a 75-mile drive from our small town. On the way there, I kept silently repeating, "We won't worry until we have to." My husband held my hand the whole drive, but I could feel how scared he was. His blue eyes gave it away every time he glanced over. My own calm started to slip a bit and for the first time we talked about what we would do if the news wasn't good. Saying "cancer" out loud felt heavy, but we agreed that if it came to that, we would face it together. We would fight with everything we had - prayer, doctors, each other. I reminded myself that I was not alone in this; I've got God's strength to lean on and He is always faithful.

In the waiting room we just sat holding hands, both of us praying silently. When they called my name, walking away from him was hard. In the procedure room, a different radiologist came in as he was covering for the usual doctor because of an emergency. He pulled up the old ultrasound images, then did a new scan to find the exact spot for the biopsy.

He stopped moving the wand. “This doesn’t look the same,” he said. He put the old and new images side by side on the screen. What had been a solid mass with veins now looked fluid-filled, like a cyst. He decided to aspirate it instead of doing the full biopsy. I watched the monitor as he guided the needle in. When he pulled back on the syringe, the whole thing just flattened and disappeared.

I looked at him, stunned, and asked, “How is that even possible?”

He smiled a little and said, “Do you believe in miracles?”

I nodded, feeling tears prick my eyes. “Yeah. I really do.”

It was such a quiet, ordinary moment that turned into something extraordinary. One minute I was bracing for the worst and the next, the thing that had scared us so much was simply gone. I still think about it when life feels uncertain. Sometimes the miracles come in ways we never expect and I am grateful, deeply grateful, for every step of it.

Tena Jolley - HR Consultant and Leadership Coach
https://www.linkedin.com/in/tena-jolley-832b7a13/

A Peace That Made No Sense

Tina Copp Stithem

I used to think that miracles were loud:

Lightning from the sky.... Angels singing... Instant, dramatic moments...

Mine wasn't like that.

Mine was slow, quiet, years in the making.

Alcohol had been a part of my life for a long time. What began as social drinking became regular, and what became regular turned into 6 months of such extreme abuse that my body could no longer survive. Addiction doesn't shout while it steals from you. It whispers.

By October of 2020, I was very, very sick.

So sick that when my husband and my adult children left for a family wedding one weekend, I stayed home. Everyone probably thought, 'Mom's just under the weather.'

I wasn't under the weather... my body was shutting down.

When my husband returned on Sunday, he knew something was very wrong. Somewhere, somehow, a decision was made that I needed the ER. The next morning, after he opened school, he came home and helped me to the car in the dark. We drove 20 miles to the hospital in Fremont, Nebraska.

When we arrived, I told him, "I can't walk." He went inside, got a wheelchair and wheeled me in. The nurse asked what was wrong. I looked up at her, barely coherent and said, "I think I have Covid." My husband quickly stepped in and calmly said, "she doesn't have Covid, she's just been very sick."

In October 2020, that was not a good way to begin an ER visit.

I remember very little after that except a doctor saying, "you've lost two pints of blood." The only conclusion they could come to was that I had likely been bleeding internally.

I remember hearing that they were trying to find a hospital to transfer me to and eventually, they found a bed at CHI Health Immanuel in Omaha. I was loaded into an ambulance in the dark.

I remember the lights of the interstate flickering past. The back of the ambulance felt mostly empty except for my gurney bolted to the floor and someone strapped into a seat in the corner. It was loud, bumpy and I was alone.

But I was not scared.

I was surrounded by a peace that made no sense.

A PEACE that did not match my condition.

A PEACE that could only come from God.

When I arrived at the hospital, they took me straight to ICU. I was hooked up to more machines than I could count. There was a long list of things wrong with me. I went through test after test, most of which I don't remember. I was mostly unconscious, and they had no idea what was wrong with me.

On the second or third day, a doctor in a white coat came into my room. As he walked in, he said, “Wow, you’re awake. You look more coherent. Yesterday we couldn’t get anything out of you; you made no sense.”

I just smiled at him.

He sat down next to me and asked me a question - I don’t remember the question but I remember my answer: “It’s too much alcohol.”

He repeated, "It’s too much alcohol?”

“Yes.”

He looked at me and said, “you just saved your life.” And they got to work.

I know in my heart that God and Jesus were in that room. I know they woke me up at that exact moment so I could say those words. I know they put that answer in me because the doctors didn’t have it.

And the peace never left.

On the 7th day, they were talking about moving me to another floor and sending me to a recovery facility.

I said, “I’m going home.”

They told me, “that’s not a good idea. You should never drink again, and you need help for that.”

I said, “No. I’m going home. I had already decided on day 1 that I am done with alcohol.”

The doctor said, “that’s easier said than done.” I looked at him and said, “Watch me,” and he said, “Okay.”

I called my husband and told him to come and get me. I could barely walk 10 steps and was using a walker, but I was going home.

October 6, 2020, is the day I count as my sobriety date. I'm not even sure if that was the first day I technically stopped drinking because I had been so sick for days before that.

But that is the day God drew a line in the sand for me.

God didn't shame me. He didn't lecture me. He didn't say, "look what you did."

He wrapped me in peace.

And that peace changed everything.

I have spent the last 5 years healing what I did to myself. And I will tell you this: it has all been about mindset and realizing just how lost I was.

God came and picked me up.

Every single day since then, He has met me exactly where I needed Him and brought the people into my life that I needed at the exact time I needed them.

I used to think miracles were rare. Now I know that miracles sometimes look like a woman who should be terrified... lying in an ambulance in total calm. Sometimes miracles look like a hospital bed. Sometimes miracles look like waking up without the chains you wore for years.

Miracles are normal and I am living proof.

Tina Copp Stithem - Faith-Led Author, Recovery & Life Encourager

https://Joingoodlife.com

https://www.facebook.com/tina.stithem

I Took The Long Way Home

Veronica Bath

I don't remember my childhood and adolescence very much; my father was a very angry man who was an alcoholic and absent most of the time. My mother wasn't very different. While she didn't drink, she wasn't present with us kids. She would escape into her crafts and her books. They both had tempers and could blow at any minute into a violent rage.

I was about 11 when my father got sick. He did try to make amends when he finally realized his fate. I had just turned 13 when he passed. This was my first experience with the death of a loved one so I looked to my family for guidance. Their solution was to "just get over it" and move on. So I stuffed my emotions down and did the best I could to move on.

While my father's death was my first, it definitely wasn't going to be the last. Over the next 7 years, I lost more than 10 close family members and several friends and classmates. I also miscarried during all of this. There was constant chaos in my life. I was heartbroken and had no one to turn to, so I toughened up just to survive.

I tried running away several times but I was pulled back each time. Somehow I had become the caretaker of the family and they couldn't survive without me. I was the youngest of the family but the most responsible one. I took care of them and all their children. While I was at odds with my mother and 2 older sisters, I just couldn't let my 5 nieces and nephews suffer.

So my boyfriend and I came home for good to take care of my mother and the children while my sisters went off to live their lives. My mother would let my oldest sister come back with a new boyfriend when she ran out of money and needed a place to stay but she refused to help out with her own children.

I did marry my boyfriend at the time but he was just another child to support. Like my father, he spent what little money he made on his addiction and whatever else he wanted, which didn't include supporting the family. Luckily I had a good paying job and the children never wanted for anything.

After our marriage, I was told by the doctors that I would never be able to have children of my own because of the damage and infections caused by the D&C done after my miscarriage. I so wanted to have my own children but eventually I accepted that caring for my sister's children had to be enough. Thankfully, the Universe had other plans. I was blessed with my first son a few years later.

It was the happiest time of my life. It felt like everything shifted and all the deep sadness just disappeared. While my family continued to cause chaos and destruction, I had created a beautiful baby boy that brought joy to the whole family. He was my miracle child.

Then about 5 years later, it all fell apart.

I was pregnant with my second child and in the middle of a divorce. All the children went back to their parents. I was heartbroken and felt beaten down but I still needed to be the caretaker to my mom and my oldest child who had also had their hearts broken and felt abandoned. The deep sadness set back in.

I met a wonderful man a few years later. We got married and he adopted my 2 sons. We built a new home with a mother-law set-up. I was laid off from my job but we decided it would be a good idea for me to be a stay-at-home mom while I worked on the next step in my life.

I had everything that I dreamed of. A supportive husband, 2 awesome boys and a spacious house in which to raise them. I was finally able to just be responsible for my own family. I was still taking care of my mother but she had her own space and we had ours.

Once the rush of getting married and building a house wore off, I started to fall into the darkness that I had been avoiding all my life. The chaos of my family had kept me so busy that I didn't have time to see how messed-up my life had become and how it had messed me up.

I was going through the dark night of the soul. I had started my spiritual awakening. I took program after program and training after training. I gained so much knowledge of my energy system and had the ability to help others so I started a small Reiki/Spiritual counseling online business.

About 6 yrs later my mom passed and I was devastated. I let go of my business so I could focus on my family. A few years later, my oldest sister passed away. Then a few years after that, my middle sister passed away. I had to be the strong one for their children and husbands plus my own family. I still hadn't faced the grief that I had been holding onto for years, I was just adding to it. There was a part of me that felt responsible for everyone else's happiness and well-being but not my own.

A few years later when my youngest was a senior in High school, I finally felt like it was time for me to move forward. I joined different programs to connect better with my Higher Self, to heal and to explore my natural healing abilities. I gained access to my ability to work with the light code to dissolve the limitation patterns held in the energetic field.

This was a miracle and a game changer. I had spent 15+ years trying to shift myself out of the deep sadness and only living in survival mode. I had tried everything:

meditation, affirmation work, persona work, energy work, etc.... but now I finally had the tool to dissolve the limiting beliefs where they were being created, at the core of my being.

I was able to heal enough where I could break free from my extended family. They only contacted me when they needed something and expected me to drop everything to come to their rescue. So, I packed up my family and we moved several states away. It took some time to finally find a place where we could settle and start rebuilding our lives but it was well worth the hassle.

While I was seeing some shift in my thinking, I wasn't really experiencing much difference in my physical reality. I was still struggling with deep sadness and thoughts of leaving this planet but now I had the tools to help me through it. In one of my darkest moments, I cried out to the Universe, "I have worked on everything you have shown me, why do I still feel like this, why is it not working for me like it does everyone else?"

The words I heard not only surprised me but confused me... Soul Embodiment. "What do you mean Soul Embodiment? Isn't that what I have been doing? I did the work and allowed the integration. Isn't that enough?" "No". So I allowed myself to sit in the confusion and trust that what I needed to do would come to me. Surrendering was new to me but I didn't really feel like I had a choice.

I was soon invited to join a program to hone my facilitation skills and a retreat before it started. I had no idea what I was in for but it felt right. At the retreat, the first thing we were asked to do was to come into the body and to describe how it felt. That was the hardest but most amazing thing that I had ever done. I have grounded, I have channeled energy, I thought I had integrated energy before, and I could feel pain and energy in my body but this was something else: it was exactly what I was looking for... Soul Embodiment.

Another miracle that truly changed everything for me was when I found that I had been doing all the work on the energetic level but missing actually releasing limitation patterns and stuck emotions in my body, causing my pain and suffering and not allowing me to manifest my desires in my physical reality.

So I created a radio show that I have turned into a program to help others do just that; to fully embody not only your soul but to live your soul truth. It has been amazing witnessing my transformation throughout this process and that of all the women I have worked with since.

I also recently discovered that my inner healer archetype that is solely responsible for my health and well-being, was carrying wounds that would not allow me to put myself and my body first. Once I did the work, awakened her and bought her fully back online, I was able to make better life choices and begin new healthy habits which were easier to implement and stick to. I am actually excited about life now and the dark thoughts of leaving this planet have vanished.

While it may not be easy to face your shadow side and the wounds of the past, it is necessary for your health and well-being. There are ways of doing this without having to re-live the trauma. I don't suggest doing it alone. I tried that for many years with not much success.

Much love and many blessings.

Veronica Bath - Alignment Alchemist, Whole Health Practitioner

https://veronica-bath.com

https://www.facebook.com/veronica.bath/

The Voice That Saves

Victoria Duarte

My father drove drunk... with me in the car. He didn't stop because he finally realized my life had meaning — he stopped because he hit a police car. "It's a miracle you're alive," my family often told me. A twist of fate, they called it - the right police car in the right place at the right time.

That wasn't my only brush with fate. In sixth grade, I usually caught the late bus home, but on some days, I walked to my aunt's house near the school. One afternoon, despite an uneasy feeling in my gut, I chose to walk. I was hungry, craving my aunt's chocolate chip cookies and eager to catch my favorite TV show. As I walked, a white van slowed beside me. My heart raced even as it drove away and then circled back. I remembered what my teachers had taught us — don't yell "help," shout "FIRE." So I screamed "FIRE" with my hands waving in the air. The commotion stirred a German Shepherd dog I had only seen pictured behind a "Beware of Dog" sign. His barking sparked a choir of neighborhood dogs, their chorus sending the van speeding away. That day taught me to trust my intuition.

In ninth grade, I went to my first unsupervised party. My mother had warned me about this particular friend, but I dismissed her concerns as overprotective. At the party, I met a boy—handsome, well-dressed, fluent in French. He said he was eighteen and asked me out on a date. I agreed, but something felt off. When he insisted on picking me up, I declined. When he suggested going to the park, I steered us to a coffee shop instead. I arrived early and bought my drink, refusing his repeated offers to buy me another. Then came that voice in my head, sharp and clear: "Don't drink that". I excused myself to the bathroom near the entrance and left. A week later, my friend called to warn me — he had raped someone she knew. Once again, my intuition had saved me.

These weren't even my biggest miracles. At the age of twenty-five, doctors told me I couldn't have children. My diagnosis, combined with necessary medications that could cause heart defects, made pregnancy nearly impossible. I was devastated. At work, the parents of my students would tell me what a wonderful mother I'd make, and I'd smile through tears, keeping my heartache hidden.

Then, one day, my mother told me a story I had never heard. Unlike the familiar tale of how my sister Linda got her name (a story that always stung since my parents had only planned to name me Jose), this was about my mother's struggle with infertility. She described her pilgrimage in Portugal, crawling on bloody knees from the Basilica of the Most Trinity to the Chapel of Apparitions, praying for the miracle of pregnancy. As a child, I had been horrified by the sight of pilgrims doing this... crying, bleeding, screaming, praying. Now, the story stirred something in me.

I worked at a Catholic school then and often lit candles in the chapel. One day, while praying for a friend in labor, trying to suppress my mixture of joy and sadness, I heard a clear voice say: "When are you going to ask about different medication?" The question cut through years of resignation and accepting doctors' verdicts as fate. I had been so focused on playing auntie to my friends' children that I had forgotten to question whether or not there might be another way.

Two years later, I went out for breakfast with a friend. My typical breakfast was a sugary drink and a bagel, but that day, I ordered two breakfasts and one to go. My friend laughed and said, "are you pregnant?" Out of curiosity, I took a pregnancy test. Much to my surprise, it was positive.

Faith comes in many forms. Sometimes, it's a mother crawling on her knees in Portugal. Sometimes, it's a voice in your head telling you to run. And sometimes, it's the courage to ask one more question when all hope seems lost.

My healthy and beautiful daughter was born in April 2008. I held my miracle in my arms at the hospital and smiled whenever a nurse asked, "how is mommy doing?" My daughter is now 16 years old, has presented at Capitol Hill a few times, and dreams endlessly about college life and all the possibilities ahead of her.

I am a mindfulness and somatic coach and the co-founder of Healing Arts Center. Through creative writing, movement, breathwork and hypnotherapy, I guide people back to their inner compass — that quiet knowing that whispers "yes" or "no." I watch clients shed the weight of others' expectations daily and rediscover what lights them up from within. They learn to trust that same voice that saves us in dire moments; only now they hear it in everyday choices.

Victoria Duarte - Somatic & Mindfulness Life Coach
https://www.healingartsva.com
https://www.instagram.com/reikivb

Miracles Are My Baseline

Vida Hill

When we think about miracles, we often seek to find the most profound and even supernatural or inexplicable experiences as examples.

Now, I have plenty of those experiences of my own to share with you. Experiences that, even if miracles feel normal to me, still made my jaw drop to the ground in awe...

...experiences that made me feel like the luckiest and most blessed person on Earth.

I can give you a list of events both big and small.

For instance:

There was that time I really craved a Crunchie chocolate bar during my day at work. That afternoon, when I got home and opened my front door, there was one lying on my lounge floor. A friend later told me he had driven past my house that day, unaware of my craving, and simply decided to drop a Crunchie chocolate bar through my cat flap as a surprise for when I got home from work.

Or when I started having really severe period pain after recurrent miscarriages. The pain radiated down my legs and I could barely walk. However, the second month in I decided to walk down to the beach in spite of the pain and I worked one of my own healing protocols on myself. Thirty minutes later the pain was gone and I haven't had period pain since - at the time of writing this it has been over 9 years. Some may call that a miracle healing. And here is the kicker, I now also have two happy and healthy young boys.

One of my most recent miracles was manifesting the house my boys and I are living in at the moment. I was absolutely desperate to find a place in which to live after separating from my ex-husband. We were still living on the same property and the relationship dynamics had turned toxic and had moved into the domestic violence space really quickly once I had made the decision to leave.

It seemed almost impossible to find a rental property as a new single mum with very little in the way of financial backing or a rental history, during a rental crisis in the area.

Then one day, a friend suggested The Wishing Game. It is a manifesting board game. I booked a session with her and met her a few days later. We made finding a new place to live a priority over all my other desires.

I followed the action steps that came through as part of the game, to anchor in this manifestation of a new home. One of them was to post on a local private rental group on Facebook again and to speak from my heart.

That evening a message landed in my inbox from a lady telling me to call her real estate agent and that I would be expected. The next day I organised a viewing of the property which just so happened to be open for inspection the following day. Within a week we had moved into our new home.

The thing is that there are so many stories like these to tell...one sounding even more magical and miraculous than the other...and recalling each story reminds me of just how blessed I really am.

However, it ultimately came back to having faith and trust that the Universe provides and always has my back.

Those moments where miracles seem to happen at the click of a finger are also those moments where I deeply surrendered into trust. I sense an innate detachment and a knowing that my needs are and will always be met.

Miracles are normal, and when you are in flow with the Universe, they are also a constant in your life.

They no longer become an elusive goal or a daydream that seems just out of your reach.

With the work I now do with women to help them to reach their fullest creative energy and expression of self, I show them the way to having miracles become their normal as well. And I can do this for you too.

I can show you how to access this innate creative power from within, to create miracles, just like mine, for yourself by tapping into the universal flow energy of creation.

You see miracles are all around you. They are in the air that you breathe and in that stroke of good luck, or in a moment that saves your life.

All that is left is to learn how to tap into them and to recognise the many moments of your life that constitute the miracles that are there for the picking already.

Afterall, who doesn't want a miracle or two every now and again?

Vida Hill - Transformational Psychic Medium & Energy Activator
www.facebook.com/vidawhill
https://vidawhill.com/

Diary Of A WILDY Child: Angel Of Light

Wildy Self

I love magical journeys. For much of my life, I have been exploring this Earth, far and wide, high and low. After deciding to leave all material possessions behind years ago, I became a true nomad, with no home, wandering through South and Central America and Southeast Asia for 3 years, solo. I found myself in Yucatan, facilitating CREATIVE Therapeutic Arts sessions at a week-long Quantum Healing Retreat held at a magnificent old Spanish hacienda in the jungle.

After the retreat, I rented a car and drove all over the peninsula scouring the area for the best cenotes (underground springs in Mexico). 'You don't know until you GO!' is my motto. I am obsessed with water and compelled to immerse myself in it whenever possible, which is how this Cenote Hunters trip was created. The pure underground-fed pools flowed as limestone karst collapsed when a massive asteroid struck Yucatan 65 million years ago.

En route to one of my favorite spots the aerial terrane map showed the sea only one block away. Turning my head to the right I spotted my glimmering muse down a narrow sandy road between two small homes. It was calling me home. I pulled in and prepared for a much needed cool down. Here, where the sand bumped up against the mystical blue-greens, the waves were very active and I could not see the sea floor as I slowly entered the powerful salty wetness. This was a tiny slice of paradise! Water to my waist, waves rolling in against my body. I felt amazingly refreshed and I rejoiced in it exclaiming out loud to the heavens "THANK GOD, I am so grateful for this life!"

At that exact moment as I stepped gently a few more shuffles forward into the deep cobalt abyss, I felt something sharp stab through my foot. The pain was outrageously intense. It felt like an ice-pick penetrated my foot deeply. Had I stepped on a large metal spike or cable? Immediately, I felt the poison coursing up my leg. A throbbing pain began to overtake my calf up to the knee as I carefully crawled out of el mar.

Immediately I wondered, HOW this could happen during a moment of UTMOST REVERENCE? WHY was I being punished by such brutal pain at such a beautiful humbling moment? HOW could my beloved treat me this way? Was I not worthy of acceptance? Had I not embodied good Karma as I had assumed? Was I cursed? I knew I was not, but could not help but wonder about the timing.

I was all alone focusing all my energy on BREATHING and keeping calm, visualizing blood flowing away from my heart to mitigate the venoms spread. Just as I asked these questions, in a split second all at once, out of nowhere a woman appeared. She walked toward me as I dragged myself toward the car on one leg, trying to keep my foot out of the sand.

My mind was doing somersaults trying to solve this puzzle and find answers and my body was focused on getting to the car, finding my tea tree oil and consulting the phone oracle about the likelihood of death due to STING RAY jab. I must have looked like a monstrocity!

She said, "Are you OK?" I was not sure, in fact. When I was able to speak, I told her my hypothesis and plan of action. She asked how she could help (in full action mode).

I needed help getting to the car and told her about the tools I required and their locations. With her compassionate presence aiding my relief, we washed my foot with drinking water, dried it and applied my tea tree oil generously while I asked the kind lady to please stay with me until I knew I was safe. She helped me into the passenger seat and propped my foot up through the open window resting it on the mirror. I began to relax and try to calm my breathing enough to slow the blood flow and read about the dangers of stingray venom.

My helper told me that she was a healer, a practitioner and teacher of Reiki and asked if she could 'work' on my foot. Her presence was already helping me feel better and I welcomed her methods and attention. As I studied the internet regarding the level of danger I may be in, my helper worked her silent magic.

Hands focused on my infliction; my hero sent me healing frequencies during which time I learned that the chances were very good that I would not suffer death and determined that there would be no hospital visit. The pain should wear off in 24 hours. As long as it stayed clear of infection, I was not in danger.

She asked how I was feeling. I took time to think clearly and assess the wound thoroughly. Unbelievably, my foot felt fine...in fact...it felt great! I was in sheer disbelief. The relief from her gift was immediate. There was NO MORE PAIN. She helped me walk back to the water's edge, as was the prescribed measure. The wound soaked in sea water for 20 minutes as we sat in the sand, our feet in the water. I asked her, "What DID you do???" She said, casually, "I called a tiny ANGEL of LIGHT to your foot and she fixed you up." I was healed and walked away with no trace of trauma.

My Angel appeared out of nowhere and then vanished again into the small village. She brought me peace in my time of desperate need. We are never truly alone.

Even when fear and pain take hold, just BREATHE and focus on THE LIGHT. Send that bright light into whatever needs healing. Hold it there and be specific with your visualization. Hold on to dear life and ENJOY THE RIDE, wherever it takes you. Nothing is a coincidence!

WILDY SELF - Guide and Mentor at WildysWorld!
https://wildysworld.com/
https://linktr.ee/wildyself

Three North Stars And The Miracles Of Restoration

Yolande Sayuri

October 30, 2023, I found myself standing in the silence of a house stripped of its furniture, toys, and photographs. It is a cruel kind of cold; the kind that reminds you that the space you once filled with a forever plan has been gutted... stolen.

Losing it all didn't happen in a single moment. It was slow. A quiet erosion. By the time my husband's addiction to prescription medication finally dismantled our world, it had taken far more than I ever thought possible. It didn't just take my person, it took our family, our home, our cars, and it took the life we had created together. It ripped the ground out from under me.

The house was gone. My home was gone. The security was gone. The man I loved was gone. The marriage did not survive. Not because I lacked understanding, or because I was unwilling to help or forgive. I understood more than most. I stayed longer than I should have. I tried, in every way I knew how, to hold things together, but there was too much damage, too much betrayal, too much hurt. All that remained was a broken heart and a bank account that sparked panic every time I checked it.

Back In 2015, I had put my business on ice, and for nearly a decade, I was a stay-at-home mom. The keeper of schedules, the maker of lunches, the personal assistant, the silent engine that kept everything running. I cared for our three children, my husband, and the home that held our dreams.

Now I was alone, in my forties, with three young children, starting over.

I cried quietly. There was no place for the kind of breakdown that stops the world, because my world couldn't stop. I had three small children who needed breakfast, playtime, an education, routine and the same story read for the hundredth time.

When you have children and your world falls apart, you don't get the luxury of falling apart with it. You become a shapeshifter. A mover. A packer. The breadwinner. The emotional anchor. All while your own heart drags behind you like a broken limb.

On the days when getting out of bed felt impossible, a small hand on my cheek became a command from the Universe. My children needed me to be healthy, to be steady, to create a sense of safety in a world that had suddenly become uncertain.

During this difficult time my three children became my North Stars. They were miracles of orientation. In the darkness of that first year, they were the only thing that stayed fixed. They did not save me, but they were the reason I chose to keep going.

My oldest became my Star of Responsibility. Watching him navigate the loss and the absence of his father's stability made something clear to me: I didn't have to be perfect, but I had to stay present.

My middle child became my Star of Joy. Even in uncertainty, she found wonder and beauty in everything. She didn't take away the pain, but she showed me where to look for light. She reminded me that while we had lost so much, we hadn't lost us. That even now, there was still beauty, still laughter, still love.

My youngest, my Star of Hope. In her simple need to be held, comforted and loved, she needed me to be calm and grounded and to give that to her, I had to become it for myself.

My children are not carrying my burden; they are the light that shows me where to step. They are the reason I stopped being a victim of the storm and became the captain of the ship.

And so, the rebuilding began...

We moved into an apartment. Smaller, humbler... but the light inside is stronger, steadier than the one we left behind.

Today I am building a hybrid career: I help authors bring their books to life through book formatting and editing, I teach English as a Second Language, and in my spare time, I return to my background as a professional behaviourist and dog trainer, helping improve animal welfare through positive dog training.

I am not a "jack of all trades," but a master of three. A diverse portfolio is adaptability...versatility. It is a testament to the fact that I am capable of everything required to keep my children safe.

A miracle is not always one grand, life-altering moment. More often, it is a thousand small ordinary ones that don't announce themselves. These moments don't look like miracles from the outside. But they are the wonders, small, steady, and essential to our daily existence;

Getting out of bed when your body feels too heavy to move.
Making breakfast when your heart is breaking.
Answering "Mom?" for the hundredth time with patience you didn't know you still had.

All, miracles.

I am forty-five. I am on my own. I am starting over, and I am the most capable version of myself I have ever known. I am not just surviving; I am creating, providing, and rising, for my children and for myself.

That is a miracle.

I have discovered a profound sense of grit and self-reliance I didn't know I possessed. This period has been one of silent transformation, forging a stronger version of myself who deeply appreciates the value of independence and the strength to build a future completely on my own terms.

And that is a Miracle.

The miracle isn't just that we survived. The miracle is the rebuilding, the restoring; An ongoing, daily act of effort, love and determination.

Yolande Sayuri Ginsberg – Book Layout Designer, ESL Tutor, Animal Behaviourist
instagram.com/yolandesayuri
yolandesayurig@gmail.com

The Meaning Of Miracles

Yolande van Niekerk

Throughout history, miracles walked a fine golden line between wonder and danger, weaving an inconceivable divine balance of ordinary and extraordinary experiences. The heavens seem to bend from impossible to possible, inexplicable, somehow plausible, welcome and yet defiant to expectations.

For many, it is undeniable evidence of a higher power. For others, it is proof of delusion.

Miracles can feel uncomfortable; sceptics treat them as relics of outdated times. Yet, miracles outlast.

Miracles show up unannounced... to overcome the odds, to ease tough times, to facilitate forgiveness, to unearth being 'stuck' and to find hope in despair; occurring in moments so personal and so perfectly timed that even doubters agree that the word 'Miracle' is most appropriate.

I understand this tension intimately and I briefly share one of my experiences here, not as proof but as an invitation to think differently.

The night I lived... and the many years it took to understand 'Why':

On the 5th of April, 1997, at 4:10 in the morning, outside Villiers in the Free State of South Africa, I was a passenger on a school bus returning home from a school camp in Natal.

We never made it home. The school bus crashed and I was trapped in the wreckage for 4 hours until rescuers successfully freed my legs by cutting through the crushed metal with the jaws of life.

During that long night, I had a near-death experience. My soul faced the choice between holding on to life or letting go. I had lost a lot of blood and I needed a transfusion but I survived. This was the first miracle I experienced from that event.

The second miracle was quieter. A month before the accident, my dad had started a new job that included medical cover. Without it, my recovery would have been much harder. After many surgeries had depleted the available insurance funds, my parents spent their savings on my rehab and recovery.

I suffered several fractures from my pelvis down to my feet. The doctor said I would probably never sit, stand or walk normally again. But today, I can do all three.

Months after my surgeries, I was learning to walk but was expected to walk with a limp forever. One day, my aunt took me to church in a wheelchair, with my crutches. Surrounded by people praying and singing, my right leg lengthened, restoring my strides.

As a teenager still recovering, on medication and having to deal with hormones, I was asked to share my miracles with the community in order to restore people's faith. I shared my experiences with local groups and small crowds, becoming, unintentionally, branded 'a miracle.' How do you honour meaning when identity forms around it?

Another girl on the same bus was paralysed and this difference stayed with me. I felt she deserved the miracle more than I did. Obligated to be loyal to a religion I was raised believing, how could I turn away from a God or a community responsible for healing me? How do you talk about these things honestly, without exaggeration or authority? How do you stay grounded when your world is shaken and you feel singled out?

What made the experience difficult was what followed in later years. When life brought cycles with no miracles, the same God provided no help, no change. Feeling let down by God when my beliefs changed, I felt disoriented by the inner upheaval. Unspoken pressure, guilt and shame shaped my adult life and relationships. I felt defective and deceived.

Seeking answers from self-help and spiritual sources, I stopped looking for miracles and tried to understand them instead. Endless questions whirled in my mind for years. Did a miracle happen to me? Why do some people experience miracles and others don't? Why does faith help some, but not others? Why do coincidences feel like holy intervention? Why can some miracles come with obligations that heal and hurt us both at the same time? What happens when meaning alters and certainty fades?

And so I learned that it's better to focus on how miracles change people and not on what they prove. Today, the old definitions of a miracle collapse quickly: "Events so impossible as to violate natural laws and expectations; only divine intervention could explain them." The more we learn, the less room there is for the supernatural. We often think, "if we can explain a miracle, it becomes less important." Yet, if we understand the science behind love, it is still love... understanding attachment doesn't make grief any less real.

Miracles help us to understand the 'meaning' assigned to events, while science explains 'how' they happen. Even in a world where we understand how things work a miracle doesn't have to break rules to matter. It's not about dramatic results, but about letting go of who we used to be. 'A miracle is something that changes how we see ourselves and our future, helping us to move toward more responsibility, care and truth.'

When someone is profoundly changed, old traumas and pain no longer control them in predictable ways. People can tap into forgiveness without an incentive and they can return from despair without a demanding narrative. Statistically improbable yet ethically far from neutral.

I share a second personal experience - an inner window of opportunity to grow up:

In November 2019, during a challenging year, I went to another 7-day meditation retreat. These gatherings were a good place to look for answers. Many people came hoping for a miracle that matched dreams, wishes and a desire for healing.

Over the years, I saw many miracles and sudden recoveries at similar events. But I also noticed something sadder: people who came with hope, only to leave disappointed and unchanged.

This contrast never left me. By then I learned to be careful about labelling healing.

Here is some background about my miracle: When I became pregnant with my daughter, I had a C-section in 2007, where a general anaesthetic was administered. Injuries from the bus accident weakened my pelvic floor, resulting in early labour at only 6 months into my pregnancy. Luckily, my doctor was able to stop it. I was prescribed Pethadine (a powerful pain medicine) and hospitalised on and off for three months. I was ordered to bed-rest lying on my sides to reach full term.

I wasn't awake to see her first breath. This absence produced hidden subconscious questions: Why was I healed enough to walk after the bus accident... but not enough to carry my child without medical intervention? Will missing her first moment affect our relationship?

A year after her birth, my marriage came to an end. At that time I was building a career in financial services, serving as a Director and shareholder in a start-up consortium of companies. Because of my level of earnings, tables turned and my ex-husband gained custody during the week. My daughter stayed with me every weekend and during holidays. I carried enormous guilt and shame about this involuntary arrangement that left me voiceless.

At the retreat, during one meditation, something unexpected happened. I found myself back in the hospital room where my daughter was born, not from a memory, but as a presence, floating near the ceiling over my bed in the hospital ward. Some might call this an out-of-body experience. I observed her first breath, her first moment and I heard her first cry as vividly as though time had collapsed upon itself.

It didn't matter if the experience was literal or symbolic. What mattered was the change it brought. For the first time, something inside me relaxed. Deep down, viscerally understanding that I was never really absent... I had been there all along! My awareness wasn't confined to my body or memory; I was there with her.

This inner miracle erased years of hidden guilt. Within a day of coming home from the retreat, my life changed in ways I could never have foreseen. Seemingly impossible circumstances dissolved; legal complications resolved; and the most wonderful of all...my daughter was able to come and live with me full-time within a month.

I still see this inner change as the greatest gift. It didn't spare me from hard times or bring a fairy-tale ending. Instead, it asked something considerably greater of me.

Helping my teenage daughter through years of mental health struggles changed everything I thought I knew about healing. What I knew wasn't what she needed; I couldn't rescue her or be her coach. I am and will always be her mom, present with her pain and my own, letting professionals help us both and trusting her wisdom. After a long, difficult time, I no longer recognised the part of me seeking answers at retreats.

Miracles don't always save us from life, sometimes they bring us back to it with more maturity.

History, religion and different worldviews have warned us about the dangers of seeing miracles as proof of special status, a right to lead or a reason to avoid responsibility. They remind us that a healthy dose of doubt is wisdom.

Traditions across cultures did not trust miracles. They saw what happens when intensity and excitement outrun humility. They understood this long before modern psychology existed. Not asking, "did anything noteworthy happen?" but instead "what kind of person did this create?" Miracles, even if impressive, were rejected as they could lead to arrogance, urgency, isolation or harm. In our instant world, this wisdom is worthy of revival.

In a crisis, arousal intensifies the meaning assigned to events, making it more likely to perceive positive outcomes as miracles. When normal thinking is rattled, we consider change and possibilities.

A real miracle tends to be paradoxical. Less dramatic over time, it does not demand faith, it resists explanation, it requires no repetition and it seeks no followers. Instead, it reveals quieter changes such as increased humility, patience, honesty and a return to daily life with more love and care.

Healthy integration of miracles happens when we no longer need a crisis or a desire to change meaning. Self-restraint is a healthy way of approaching a miracle. This lets us stay open without being naïve. Experiences can be meaningful without elevated status, special treatment or ease.

A well-integrated miracle increases care, patience and humility. If not grounded in truth, it results in increased urgency, special treatment, inflated self-importance and unhealthy amplification of status.

Even with all we know, miracles endure. It is the golden thread occasionally revealing itself in our human story. Humans are unpredictable, with unique experiences in an ever-changing world, giving meaning to circumstantial patterns when disrupted and changed in inconceivable ways.

Miracles offer no guarantees and cannot compete with reason or be pinned down by probabilities. The meaning they bring to life can't be forced, proven or repeated. It has to be lived, moment by moment.

Life sometimes gives us no reason and no miracle to improve...we do it anyway, that is a miracle in itself.

Perhaps the most dangerous misunderstanding about miracles is the belief that they lead to easier outcomes. Genuine miracles seem to make us braver, wiser and more responsible than we ever expected.

Yolande van Niekerk
https://thanksyolande.com

Just An Ordinary Morning

Zora Hanáčková PhD

In the winter of 1998, I lived in a suburb of Bratislava, Slovakia. This part of the capital had once been a separate village, later swallowed by the expanding city and filled with new high-rise apartment buildings. It took a 25-minute bus ride along the highway to reach the Academy of Sciences where I worked as a young scientist.

On the way from the suburb to the highway, there was a dangerous curve where far too many accidents occurred. The traffic sign demanding a reduced speed when exiting the highway and turning toward the suburb, was often ignored – with tragic consequences, especially on frozen winter roads.

Picture a typical mid-December weekday morning… the bus was overcrowded. I stood at the very front, right beside the driver. People were wrapped in their own thoughts, silent, disconnected from one another.

The weekend before, I had completed an advanced energy healing course. I received a powerful attunement to the next level, allowing me to use specially programmed sacred geometry symbols – one of them designed to harmonize situations and spaces. I had only started working with it that week, practicing quietly in different circumstances.

It was a dull, uneventful morning. The bus stopped before merging onto the highway.

Suddenly I heard a distinct voice in my head, clearly instructing me: "Switch the harmonizing symbol on!"

Activating the symbol took only a second. I had no idea why I had to do it. Everything that followed happened both incredibly fast and in strange slow motion – as if every fraction of a second stretched wide open.

A black Mercedes was approaching the curve from the highway far too quickly. There was no way the driver could slow down in time. The curve was a trap waiting to close.

The drowsy atmosphere inside the bus disappeared. Every pair of eyes locked onto the unfolding scene.

"He's a goner," the driver muttered under his breath.

We all saw what was coming. We collectively held our breath, bracing for the inevitable.

And then I felt it...

As the car entered the curve, a sharp surge like a lightning bolt shot through my body – entering through the crown of my head and bursting out from my solar plexus. In that same suspended moment, brakes screeched, the car swerved violently – and against all the laws of Newtonian physics, it landed back on all four wheels. It stabilized on the wet road, passed the curve safely and continued driving as if nothing had happened.

Someone's Guardian Angel must have worked overtime.

The stunned bus driver shouted, "That's... impossible!"

The entire bus exhaled at once, relief flooded the space. People began talking over each other, animated, amazed, laughing, connecting.

And I quietly looked upward and winked at my light-being friends.

Grateful doesn't fully capture what I felt.

Grateful for the divine assistance.
Grateful for the course and the attunement.
Grateful for being at the right place at the right time.
Grateful for being allowed to serve as a channel for what was needed.
Grateful for saving a man I would never meet.
Grateful for his family not receiving devastating news just before Christmas.
Grateful for the collective relief that softened everyone's morning.
Grateful for what I learned about energy work in those few extraordinary seconds.

Because if you are a healer or if you work with energy, you know. We are not the ones "doing" the healing. We are simply channels for something greater that flows through us. And to me, that is a profound honor.

At that time, I didn't speak openly about doing energy work. As a scientist, that would have been an unacceptable revelation. So I never told this story to anyone. It lived silently inside me; alongside a truth I wasn't yet ready to defend.

Who would have believed me anyway?

Many years have passed since that ordinary morning. There have been countless trainings, certifications and life changes. I stopped hiding my work. For nearly 25 years now, I have been a full-time energy therapist and educator.

In my practice, I blend structured scientific thinking with advanced energy work and my natural empathic abilities. I focus on helping people release trauma gently, safely and without retraumatization.

I helped hundreds of clients release the most painful experiences of their lives, reprogram their limiting beliefs and dissolve deeply imprinted subconscious patterns. I love what I do and for me there is nothing more fulfilling than witnessing my clients transforming right before my eyes, rebuilding their resilience, serenity and inner stability.

It is now my mission to teach other energy workers how to help their clients release trauma with clarity and confidence. Because when enough of us return to inner equanimity, that calm begins to ripple outward, creating greater peace and harmony for all of us.

And sometimes, it all begins on just an ordinary morning.

Zora Hanáčková PhD – Trauma Release Energy Therapist
https://www.freedomflowenergywork.com
https://www.linkedin.com/in/zora-hanackova-phd

About Soul Purpose Publishing

Dina Marais is the founder of Soul Purpose Publishing and Coaching, an 9-time International Bestselling Author, an Independent Publisher of 6 international bestsellers, and a Prosperity Alignment Coach.

Soul Purpose Publishing and Coaching consists of an intimate team of professionals who give personal attention to their clients. Their values are to inspire and empower the hearts and minds of writers/authors and readers.

The mission of Soul Purpose Publishing and Coaching is to serve conscious entrepreneurs to elevate their brands, authority, credibility, impact and income by becoming bestselling authors, as well as to manifest their highest visions through energetic alignment.

Whether you wish to contribute a chapter to a multi-author book, write your solo book, get your manuscript published, or have the desire to publish the stories of your community, Soul Purpose Publishing is equipped to provide you with excellent service.

As a Prosperity Alignment Coach, Dina supports entrepreneurs in manifesting their dream goals through practices of self-love, energetic alignment, and effective strategies, as described in The Prosperity Generator.

Learn more about how to work with Dina and her team to support you in fulfilling your soul purpose.

www.dinamarais.com

www.ingramcontent.com/pod-product-compliance
Lightning Source LLC
LaVergne TN
LVHW020704110826
845149LV00012B/2105
9798989656097